HISTORIC
DISASTERS
—— IN ——
SOUTHEAST
MINNESOTA

HISTORIC
DISASTERS
── IN ──
SOUTHEAST
MINNESOTA

STEVE GARDINER

THE
History
PRESS

Published by The History Press
Charleston, SC
www.historypress.com

Copyright © 2022 by Steve Gardiner
All rights reserved

Front cover: courtesy of the Goodhue County Historical Society.
Back cover: courtesy of the Winona County Historical Society.

First published 2022

Manufactured in the United States

ISBN 9781467150941

Library of Congress Control Number: 2021952407

*To those who suffered as a result of the natural disasters in this book,
and to those who stepped up to help.*

CONTENTS

PREFACE

The three major events described in this book happened over a span of seventy-five years. Many changes took place in society during that period, and one that is easily noticeable in the pages of this book is the dynamic nature of the newspaper business. Throughout those years, publications opened and closed. Newspapers combined and changed names, some revising their flag several times during the years included in this book.

As one example, the *Red Wing Republican* opened in 1857. It became the *Daily Republican* in 1885, just before the *Sea Wing* incident. In 1940, it merged with the rival *Daily Eagle* and put out the first edition of the *Daily Republican Eagle* on November 25, just two weeks after the Armistice Day Blizzard. References used in that section will change, even as the reporting is still covering events that were current for that tragedy. Then, in 1969, the paper dropped *Daily* from its name. These changes are still happening as newspapers merge, change ownership and, sadly, close.

The history of the Red Wing newspapers is representative of what happened to newspapers throughout the region in those eight decades. The papers in Winona went through three different names, and the papers in Minneapolis, St. Paul, Rochester and other communities in the region went through similar changes. Readers will notice the different names among the three sections of this book.

ACKNOWLEDGEMENTS

A fter retiring as a high school English teacher, I moved to Minnesota and took a job as a news reporter with the *Red Wing Republican Eagle* and RiverTown Multimedia. Many thanks to editor Anne Jacobson for giving me that opportunity and for assigning me to write stories for a special weather edition. Those short articles became the ideas for the three parts of this book. Also, thanks to media editor Mike Brun for daily inspiration and assistance as I made the transition from teacher to reporter. Both of them are amazing professionals in the news business.

Many thanks to Jim O'Rourke, owner of O'Rourke Media Group, who purchased RiverTown Multimedia in 2020. He granted permission to use photos and parts of the articles that had appeared in the weather issue.

Thanks to John Rodrigue, acquisitions editor for The History Press, who saw the articles in the weather issue, contacted me and invited me to write a book on these three subjects and gave me excellent advice throughout the process of turning these events into a book. Rick Delaney offered valuable comments regarding style and consistency as the copyeditor.

Historical research is a team project, and I want to thank Afton Esson with the Goodhue County Historical Society in Red Wing for his help in locating articles and photos for all three stories included here. Also, many thanks to Afton for helping with a long list of other articles throughout my three years at RiverTown Multimedia.

Walt Bennick, with the Winona County Historical Society, introduced me to the Winona Newspaper Project, an incredible resource, and helped me get photos of the flood and blizzard in that community. Krista Lewis, at the History Center of Olmsted County, provided access to photos and articles about Rochester and the surrounding area, especially regarding the flood. Don Schwartz with the Lake City Historical Society helped locate photos and information about the *Sea Wing* disaster.

My wife, Peggy, accompanied me on many travels around the region to gather information for both newspaper articles and this book, making each of those journeys more enjoyable and meaningful.

Finally, I'd like to thank the Mississippi River and Lake Pepin, where the river takes a break and slows down for a few miles, for being such incredible places to live and work. The river and the surrounding bluff lands are home to many species of birds and wildlife, as well as the water and weather that create the natural beauty of this region and make it an interesting place to call home.

INTRODUCTION

The three major events in this book—the *Sea Wing* wreck, the Armistice Day Blizzard and the flood of 1965—happened in July 1890, November 1940 and April 1965, respectively. They span not only a broad number of years but also a cycle of months on the calendar. They involve a variety of weather conditions: wind, water, rain, snow, cold, hail, blizzard and flood. While Southeast Minnesota isn't the only place with such conditions, the weather is certainly a frequent topic of discussion in the area. These three tragedies, though they are beyond most people's memories, are part of the regional history. The challenges these events presented to people living here and the stories of how people overcame those challenges are the foundations of many local legends.

They are examples of the natural environment taking control and causing extensive damage to property and human lives. In two cases—those of the *Sea Wing* and the Armistice Day Blizzard—nature moved in quickly, taking people by surprise and making them react instantly to the danger they faced. In the other case, the Flood of 1965, nature moved slowly but relentlessly, forcing locals to endure days and weeks of anxiety and fear.

While these are stories of statistics—of inches of snow, of feet of floodwater, of deaths and damage inflicted—they are also stories of human beings. These stories show how weather can make us feel helpless but can also bring out the best in our collective willingness to help others. The tragedies recounted here had a high cost in terms of dollars, injuries and death, as well as human emotion endured, but they also created change in terms of improved weather forecasting, new safety regulations and funding for the prevention of flooding and other disasters.

They are stories of human tragedy that provide us with powerful lessons.

PART I

THE WRECK OF THE *SEA WING* (1890)

1

SUNDAY AFTERNOON ON THE RIVER

I t was supposed to be an afternoon outing on the Mississippi River, a chance to enjoy friends, music and a boat ride. Then, tornado-strength winds crashed down on Lake Pepin and turned the event into the worst marine tragedy in Minnesota history.

Captain David Wethern, part owner of the *Sea Wing*, a 109-ton stern wheeler, usually used his boat for moving timber on the river, but on occasion he arranged passenger outings. He had advertised that on the afternoon of July 13, 1890, he would be loading passengers on the *Sea Wing* and on an attached barge called the *Jim Grant*. He planned to leave his home in Diamond Bluff, where he owned a general store, then make stops in Trenton and Red Wing before heading downriver to Lake City for festivities at the First Regiment, Minnesota National Guard summer camp located two miles south of Lake City. Plenty of the soldiers were from Red Wing, so family members and sweethearts were anxious to see them. Afternoon activities would include a band concert, cannon firing and soldiers marching in formation.

Wethern took out an ad in a Red Wing newspaper, announcing, "Hawkins full string band has been engaged to furnish the music" and "tickets for the round trip 50 cents."

Temperatures had been warm, and an afternoon excursion on beautiful Lake Pepin seemed like a pleasant way to enjoy the day. The lake, the largest on the Mississippi River, formed thousands of years ago when the Chippewa River in Wisconsin dropped tons of sand into the Mississippi River, creating

Camp Lakeview, the destination of the *Sea Wing* excursion, was two miles south of Lake City on the shore of Lake Pepin. *Courtesy of the Goodhue County Historical Society.*

A crowd of finely dressed passengers gathers on the decks of the *Sea Wing. Courtesy of the Goodhue County Historical Society.*

a natural dam that exists to this day. The dam holds the river, slowing it down to a negligible current and making it an ideal location for a Sunday boat ride. Any cool breezes off the lake would be a welcome respite.

According to Jean Chesley in an unpublished manuscript in the Goodhue County Historical Society files, Captain Wethern, age thirty-seven, left Diamond Bluff at about eight in the morning with a crew of ten men. The *Sea Wing* and the attached barge stopped in Trenton and picked up 22 passengers, then gained 165 more in Red Wing. They enjoyed the journey to Lake City and the afternoon at the military camp.

"The day was intensely hot with low barometric pressure and, toward evening, threatening storm clouds began to gather," Chesley wrote. "The boat had been scheduled to start back at four o'clock in the afternoon, but passengers entreated the captain to stay longer in order to prolong their pleasant visit with the boys at camp."

In an article in the *Ensign*, the quarterly magazine of United States Power Squadrons, America's Boating Club, Dean R. Crissinger noted: "There was gaity and laughter among the excursionists, and there was dancing on the barge. Lake City had created a carnival spirit with popcorn, lemonade and hamburger stands. People were carrying balloons and a band was heard playing lively music. It seems that there was so much excitement over the visit to the camp that little attention was paid to the ominous weather situation that was developing."

According to most reports, the Sea Wing was scheduled to return at 4:00 p.m., following a band concert. The festivities had been fun, and many of the passengers wanted to stay to watch the dress parade by the soldiers, which would be over at about 7:00 p.m. Wethern agreed, and in the intervening time, rain and wind moved in. Wethern waited an extra hour, thinking the rain would pass, before loading the boat and setting out for Red Wing at about 8:00 p.m.

As the steamer departed, additional winds and some rain sent many passengers, especially many of the women and children, inside the ship's cabin, a move that would soon become significant. The men gathered on the deck and in the barge *Jim Grant*.

Other steamboat men had advised Wethern to hug the Minnesota shore, and he planned to do so, but he knew he would have to go around two points, Central Point and an extended point labeled on various maps Long Point, Sand Point and Point au Sable ("Sand Point" in French). As he rounded the two points, he changed his mind and angled across the lake toward the Wisconsin shore.

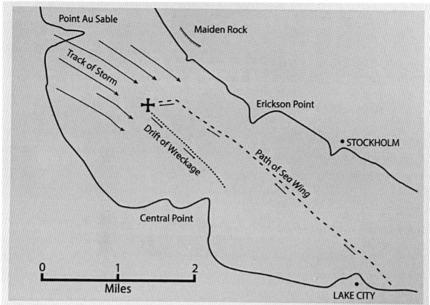

Dr. Thomas A. Hodgson, an expert yachtsman who grew up on Lake Pepin, has studied the *Sea Wing* accident and created this map of the steamer's course.

Dr. Thomas A. Hodgson created this map of the route taken by Captain Wethern and the *Sea Wing* on July 13, 1890, showing the path of travel, the turn into the storm and the drifting after it capsized. *Courtesy of the Goodhue County Historical Society.*

"The wind was blowing up the lake, a little off the Minnesota side, I think," Wethern said in the Crissinger article. "I held her for Maiden Rock Point to get her under the bluff and follow the bend. We were not quite up to the Maiden Rock Point when I saw the squall coming off the Minnesota shore. I turned the boat so as to meet the squall head on. When I was making the turn to meet the storm, she listed some, but rode up again after she got square into the wind. We ran that way straight toward the Minnesota shore for several minutes."

An article in the *Illustrated American* of August 9, 1890, only three weeks after the accident, explained that while Wethern was making this move across the lake, powerful winds swooped in and took control of the boat.

The article noted that "the steamers that ply the upper Mississippi—and the Sea Wing was no exception—are not built to weather a gale. Owing to the shallowness of the waters near shore, the draught of the steamers is light; they are smooth-keeled, and their bulk and weight are almost entirely above water-line. Their engines are not powerful, and they present a huge surface above the water to resist the blast of a storm."

Steamers were designed to move in shallow water, to avoid the sandbars and snags that plagued early travel on the Mississippi River. Some pilots claimed they could travel in as little as fourteen inches of water, and some said they could run a steamer with nothing but a "heavy dew."

In a 1930 article in the *Minneapolis Tribune*, Milt Davis explained the problems faced by the steamers working the Mississippi River, noting that during the time of the *Sea Wing* disaster, wrecks on the river were not a rarity. Many hazards awaited steamers, including snags, fires, explosions and, as in the case of the *Sea Wing*, storms.

"Snags waited like marauders for their victims," Davis wrote. "They were imbedded in the river bed, while jagged roots thrust upward. If the keen-eyed pilot failed to read aright the little danger signals that ripples and shadows might cast, the boat would bear down upon the snag. It's hull would be ripped and torn, and the helpless craft and its passengers would be in desperate plight."

Then, as steamers, there was the constant threat coming from fires burning inside the boats. The boats were wooden, with what was called "gingerbread" ornamentation.

The *Sea Wing*, with the barge *Jim Grant* attached near the port bow, cruises on Lake Pepin. *Courtesy of the Goodhue County Historical Society.*

Gary Majchrzak of Lake City built this 1/64 model of the *Sea Wing*. It is on display in the small historical museum at the Lake City Marina. *Photo by Steve Gardiner.*

"Smoke-stacks, running from the boiler-room high over the top deck were often inadequately insulated where they passed through the flooring," Davis wrote. "Fires built of pitch-soaked wood roared in the furnaces. The stack often became red hot. Wood around them caught fire—and too often that meant the whole boat and its passengers and crew were doomed."

STRAIGHT-LINE WINDS

According to a 2014 article by Curt Brown in the *Minneapolis Star Tribune*, the passengers were in close quarters inside the *Sea Wing*. It was 135 feet long and 16 feet wide with a 22-foot-high pilothouse.

"Straight-line winds began to whip Lake Pepin with waves swelling from six to eight feet," Brown wrote. "The barge rocked violently behind the Sea Wing, whose crew cut the line connecting the boats—figuring they'd fare better, lurching and rocking on their own."

Weather reports of the day noted that a tornado struck Lake Gervais and Kohlman Lake near St. Paul that afternoon, killing several people and doing extensive damage to houses and property. Trees were uprooted and houses damaged in Hastings. A 1989 story in the *Minneapolis Tribune* reported that the same wind hit sixty miles per hour and did extensive damage to houses and trees in Red Wing, as well as flattening corn and grain crops in the area. Captain Wethern, the crew and passengers of the *Sea Wing* would not have had any warning of those earlier events upriver. No system for forecasting or reporting weather existed on that fateful day.

The straight-line wind that roared in hit the broad side of the *Sea Wing* as well as the side of the *Jim Grant*. It rocked them both, throwing some of the barge passengers into the water.

The *Sea Wing* listed, then, as the *Illustrated American* explained, "righted herself for a moment, but an instant later she keeled over and lay helpless, the great waves breaking over her. She drifted a short way back to the point and then sank, with most of those on board. The barge had meanwhile broken loose from the Sea Wing and floated down opposite Lake City where about twenty people who were still on board were rescued."

The *Red Wing Republican* reported that the first wind had tipped the boat enough that passengers were thrown across the cabin to the lower side. The second wind fully capsized the *Sea Wing*, trapping many inside. Those who were thrown out or managed to get themselves out of the cabin climbed onto the upturned bottom of the boat. Some were able to find life preservers or other floating debris to hold, but many were "swallowed up in the merciless lake."

In her unpublished report, Chesley stated that the barge may have been separated from the *Sea Wing* by being cut loose by a crew member or by the powerful forces of the wind that battered both vessels. She wrote that all aboard the barge were saved, but the scene was very different inside the capsized *Sea Wing*.

"Many were imprisoned within the cabin," Chesley wrote. "Others were injured or unable to swim. Some, thrown overboard, saved their lives by securing planks, life preservers or other debris to cling to until rescued. Many unrecorded deeds of heroism took place that dark night on the lake."

Even the captain found himself in a harrowing situation. Crissinger, in the *Ensign*, quoted Wethern as saying, "I found myself in the water inside the pilot house. I put my feet against the wheel and pushed myself out through the glass and sash and swam to the surface."

Members of the Minnesota National Guard work to recover bodies the day after the wreck. *Courtesy of the Goodhue County Historical Society.*

Lake Pepin, normally quiet and peaceful in the evenings, was alive with the screams of men, women and children who hadn't been trapped inside the cabin. They were struggling in the waves. Several of the women fought against the long dresses they had worn for the festive occasion. Occasional lightning strikes gave glimpses of the frantic activity in the water.

"At first the water around them was dotted with people struggling for life, but in ten minutes there was nothing to see on the continuing high sea of waves," reported the *Red Wing Republican* on Monday, July 14, 1890.

The scene was a shock for anyone who witnessed it, and one unnamed survivor told the *Illustrated American*: "Here and there could be seen the white dress of some poor woman or child. One poor creature I saw go down clinging to her child whom she had been trying to save. The mother—for mother she evidently was had fastened a life-preserver about her waist, and with its aid was trying to keep herself and child afloat until help could reach them. Suddenly I saw the woman release the hold she had upon the child and sink beneath the water. She did not rise again, and the child soon followed its mother."

WAVES AND WATER

As many as twenty-five passengers managed to climb onto the bottom of the upturned *Sea Wing*, hoping that would save them. But, as the *Republican* reported, as the storm seemed to settle down, the boat rolled again, onto its side, casting those clinging to the hull again into the dark water.

"The men hung on the railing in danger each moment of being washed away by the waves," said the *Republican*. "One man observed the forms of two women wedged in between a stationary seat and the boat's side, both pale in death. As the lightning gleam lit up their upturned faces, another saw two little girls floating past him as he hung with desperate efforts to the steamer's side and still another man observed a man floating near him, his body encased in a life preserver, but cold in death."

The *Jim Grant* had drifted toward Central Point, just above Lake City. When it moved closer to shore, a few passengers managed to reach land and headed toward Lake City, looking for help. One of them, Harry Mabey, ran to the fire hall in Lake City and rang the alarm bell.

As soon as the alarm sounded, a number of people from Lake City "hastened to Oscar Peterson's boat yard, took skiffs and started for the scene

National Guardsmen, standing on the barge *Jim Grant*, secure the listing *Sea Wing*, seen with holes chopped in the main cabin roof. *Courtesy of the Goodhue County Historical Society.*

27

of the wreck," reported the *Lake City Graphic* on July 15. Every boat and every person available joined the rescue effort.

"They did noble service and are entitled to great credit for bravery and courage," noted the *Graphic*. "The waves were rolling many feet high, and those who went took their own lives in their hands in the undertaking."

As many as twenty people were brought ashore alive; then came the boatloads of dead bodies. Those with medical training tried to save any who were still living, but the nature of the wreck, the overturning of the *Sea Wing* with so many inside, filled everyone with fear.

The quick response of the citizens of Lake City resulted in many lives being saved, reported the *Illustrated American*. When members of the National Guard arrived, "Major Fitzgerald, surgeon of the regiment, took charge of the hospital corps and of the arrangements for handling the dead. Body after body, of men, women, and children, in some cases almost of whole families, was taken from the water, some of them alive, others unconscious, but more dead."

"Then came the big job," said Harry Mabey in the Crissinger article. "I don't know how many—eighty or ninety it seems to me—women and girls were all caged up in the cabin like so many drowned rats, and couldn't get out. We started chopping the side of the boat, removing the bodies and laying them along the shore."

SOME PASSENGERS HAD BEEN able to swim to shore, including a couple who made it to the Wisconsin side. According to the *Illustrated American*, "The bodies of those who went down with the steamer were taken out of the cabin through a hole cut in the pilot-house and through the cabin doors. Believing that some bodies were still to be found in the half-dismantled wreck, General Mullen ordered the tearing away of the upper works of the vessel and the pushing of the wreck further toward the shore, where she was righted."

The rescue efforts continued through the night and into the next day. By morning, more than fifty bodies had been removed and taken ashore. The work continued, because everyone knew there were many more dead and there was still hope of finding some alive.

Crissinger told the story of one young man who worked for thirteen hours straight, searching through the wreckage. He looked at each body that was pulled out, searching for his girlfriend, who had been on the boat.

"Later in the afternoon, a dispatch was received at the shore addressed to the anxious soldier," Crissinger wrote. "He tore it open eagerly, read the contents, and then fell on the sandy beach insensible. The dispatch informed him that the girl he loved had missed the boat by five minutes and was safely at home with her friends."

There were many stories of those who were spared on that dark and fearful night. One such account involved seventeen-year-old Robert "Boze" Adams, son of Dr. John Adams of Lake City. He and another boy from Red Wing, George Seavers, had ended up in the water together, according to the *Illustrated American*. They secured three life jackets together and held onto them. They simply rode with the waves rather than fight with them and drifted a mile downstream past Lake City. Then the wind changed and blew them in the other direction until they at last reached Frontenac, seven miles above Lake City.

In 1930, Seavers told the *Minneapolis Tribune* that when the boat rolled the second time, he had jumped into the water and was stunned for a moment but then tried reaching out. "In a flash of lightning, I saw something in front of me and grabbed it," Seavers remembered. "It was a two-foot plank. Boze Adams was near, and he also grabbed the plank. We clung to it together. Some life preservers floated by, and we seized a couple of them. I put an arm through the strap of Boze's and he did the same through mine."

When they drifted to shore, they heard a voice asking the time. Another voice said it was two o'clock. They had been in the water for nearly six hours.

"We were too weak to stand up, and we lay down, partly on the beach, partly in the water," Seavers said.

Others helped them move away from the water and find a place to recover. At noon, Seavers got on the train to head home.

2

A WAVE OF SHOCK AND REVULSION

Minneapolis Tribune reporter had been visiting friends in Lake City that day. He had been sitting outside in the yard, talking, when the winds arrived. He said the wind struck suddenly, driving all the friends inside, where they sealed windows and shutters. As they were closing the house they could hear trees crashing outside and objects blown against the side of the house. The storm lasted about half an hour, according to the reporter, who then went outside and spent the night talking to people who were coming ashore from the wreckage and those involved in the rescue attempts.

Not long after the storm ended, the reporter went to the dock in Lake City and talked with the captain of the steamer *Ethel Howard*. The reporter asked if he was going to take the steamer out to look for survivors, but the captain said he wasn't going to run the risk of losing his boat "in order to look for dead people out on the lake," although he did eventually get involved and delivered as many as fifty bodies to Red Wing the following morning.

The *Tribune* reporter said that at least a dozen rowboats headed out from Lake City in search of survivors and bodies. He also explained that apparently no one was killed in Lake City, but that the Collins Brothers saw and planing mill was demolished and that the roof of the opera house was removed. Other businesses and homes were damaged.

He ended his report by stating that by 1:30 a.m., sixty-two bodies had been laid out on shore.

Survivors were brought to the Lyon Hotel in Lake City. *Courtesy of the Goodhue County Historical Society.*

FOR MANY AREA RESIDENTS, waiting to learn the fate of family members and loved ones was the hardest part. Hours of anxiety tortured them. One letter from the Goodhue County Historical Society files illustrates the pain this waiting caused.

H.L. Keller waited, hoping he would hear news about his niece Eliza Crawford before he contacted her father, W.J. Crawford. By Tuesday morning, July 15, Keller had decided he needed to send a letter. He spoke of the tragedy on Lake Pepin and said that Eliza and another girl had been on the boat. The other girl was found dead, but there was no word about Eliza.

"Eliza is among the missing ones & has not yet been found," he wrote. "I was up all last night & today & have not as yet been able to find her. I entertain no hopes whatever of her safety."

He told Crawford that she might be found soon or that it could take days, but he would send news as he could. "There are whole families lost. As far as known there were only five females saved. There were life preservers on the boat but few availed themselves of them," he wrote, then added, "There is mourning in Red Wing as nearly all were from there."

Keller promised to send Eliza's belongings home and reflected what must have been the attitude of many in the Red Wing and Lake City area when he wrote: "God only knows the sorrow it has and will cause. We mourn not as those who have no hope. Liza was a good girl & has made many friends in so short a time. You do not know what a painful task this is. Such a disaster has never befallen this country."

"THE SUDDEN AND TERRIBLE end to the July excursion of the Sea Wing sent a wave of shock and revulsion reverberating through Minnesota and the nation," wrote Frederick Johnson, author of the book *The* Sea Wing *Disaster: Tragedy on Lake Pepin*, in an article in *Minnesota History*. "Ninety-eight were dead. Whole families had been killed. Of the fifty-seven females on board, fifty had drowned."

Johnson also examined the question of how the *Jim Grant* and *Sea Wing* were disconnected. He noted that there were many conflicting reports on what happened and when the separation occurred. One report, Johnson said, recounted someone on the barge calling for the lines to be cut. One account said a deckhand used an axe to cut the lines. Another report stated that passengers had cut the lines.

A booklet produced for attendees at a memorial service held in Red Wing on July 25 contained a summary of the events of twelve days before. The summary stated that after the *Sea Wing* had been capsized by the wind, someone cried out, "Cut the barge loose," and an employee of the boat cut the ropes, leaving the barge and boat to float to shore on their own.

The day after the accident, the *Republican* reported that when the *Sea Wing* overturned, it pulled the *Jim Grant* down to the extent that the water was at the edge of the barge sides, threatening to take it and the forty or fifty passengers inside down as well.

"The more cool headed, however, secured control and cutting the hawsers which held the barge to the boat, it floated away from the [*Sea*

Wing], drifting about in the lake seemingly at the mercy of the waters," the *Republican* stated. "It was a terrible experience on that barge. The waves rolled high above its top, and over it completely deluging the occupants at times, and it was only by the greatest exertion that most of them were kept from becoming panic stricken and causing that, also, to capsize. Finally, a favorable wind drifted the barge near to shore, and the occupants were gotten off in safety."

An initial report in the *St. Paul Pioneer Press* said the barge had been cut away, but a second report the following day stated that the lines broke when the *Sea Wing* capsized. Johnson also noted that Wethern himself changed sides on the issue.

Three days after the incident, Wethern told the *St. Paul Dispatch* that "the barge was not cut loose until the steamer capsized and then only to save it from being swamped also." Johnson then explained that, thirty-six years later, Wethern said in an interview that the *Sea Wing* would not have flipped if the ropes connecting the barge had not been cut.

RAIN AND WIND

In a newsletter for the Minnesota Military Museum, Johnson captured the storm and *Sea Wing* wreck from the viewpoint of the soldiers at Camp Lakeview. The camp was a temporary site for the summer, so it consisted of tents with no permanent structures. As the storm approached, the soldiers made hasty preparations to face the strong winds.

"For a moment all was still as death. Men rushed from their tents with axes and hatchets to drive in their tent pins. In less than one minute the cyclone struck us with all its terrific force," according to a regiment history report. "The hospital tent went up like a balloon and then came down on its occupants like a big wet cloth that it was. The air was filled with flying tent poles, tent pins, fence boards, and everything moveable moved. Not a light was burning in the camp, and between the flashes of lightning the angry waves of Lake Pepin could be seen rolling mountain high."

Colonel William Bend, in charge of Camp Lakeview, had chosen to set up the summer encampment at Lake City because he found that when he held training at Fort Snelling, employers often kept their workers on the job during the day, preventing them from being fully involved in the training. By moving the camp away from the Twin Cities, Bend hoped to keep the troops more isolated.

The storm had soaked everything in camp. Clothing, blankets, food and medical supplies were wet and damaged. The camp surgeon, Captain William H. Caine from Stillwater, and Reynolds J. Fitzgerald went into Lake City, hoping to find some supplies. What they found was a town with more than thirty buildings damaged or destroyed. It was then that they learned about the wreck of the *Sea Wing*.

They sent word to the camp asking for assistance. Then Caine and Fitzgerald headed for Central Point north of Lake City, where they assisted in the recovery of the dead throughout the night, setting up a makeshift morgue on the shore.

Major Arthur P. Pierce, a field officer from Red Wing, took control of the rescue operations. Soon after, Minnesota adjutant general John H. Mullen from Wabasha arrived at the scene and, in the morning, brought in Artillery Battery A and had them shoot cannons into the water, hoping to raise any bodies underwater. They fired several shots on Monday and on Tuesday used dynamite to shock the water.

The booklet for the memorial service noted that the steamer *Ethel Howard* arrived in Red Wing about six o'clock Monday morning, delivering forty-two bodies. By noon, another steamer, the *Nettie Durant*, had brought eight more.

On Monday afternoon, two steamers were able to move the *Sea Wing* into such a position that the cabin could be opened. Rescuers were able to locate fifteen more bodies and deliver them to Red Wing. Over the next two days, several boats maintained a watch for bodies in the area.

On Wednesday, the steamer *Menomonee* passed near the site of the wreck, and the movement caused a body to surface. With that event, the *Menomonee* made several more passes and was able to locate thirty-one more bodies, leaving only one missing person unaccounted for.

On Thursday morning, the ninety-eighth and final body was found, and the gruesome recovery work at Lake Pepin was finished.

Red Wing coroner John E. Kyllo took charge of the bodies, and as they were delivered to the undertaking room of Swanson and Allen, a "heartbreaking spectacle followed," reported the *Republican*. "Wives came searching for husbands, husbands came searching for wives, mothers and fathers looking for children, and the anguish was heart breaking in the extreme. As fast as

The *Netta Durant* steamer seen pulling the *Sea Wing* closer to shore so rescuers could search for bodies. *Courtesy of the Goodhue County Historical Society.*

they were identified, they were removed to be cared for and others brought in for inspection."

Seventy-seven of the dead were from Red Wing, and church bells rang constantly over the next several days as forty-four victims were buried on Tuesday alone.

"In Red Wing business was practically suspended for four days," according to the summary in the memorial service booklet. "Upon the arrival of the remains of victims they were taken in charge by the coroner until properly identified, and then delivered to the relatives, friends, or associations claiming them for burial. Funerals began Monday evening and continued through that and three following days. The tolling of bells was almost incessant, and some funeral procession was traversing the streets every hour."

Funeral services for ten victims were held in Diamond Bluff and ten more in Trenton. In Red Wing, three services were held on Monday, forty-four on Tuesday, fifteen on Wednesday and nine on Thursday.

CALM AND QUIET

On Friday, July 25, a memorial service was held in Red Wing. Some five thousand people attended to console one another and to try to make some sense of the devastation that had racked the community. They came to hear speakers like Red Wing attorney and politician Osee Matson Hall and the Reverend W.C. Rice—and, perhaps, to gain some understanding of why such a tragic event had happened.

"Ninety-eight perished," said Hall. "Of the two hundred and fourteen who on that cyclonic day wrestled with the storm, ninety-eight are gone forever. We knew them well. Their faces, names, lives were familiar to us all. Some of them were the pioneers of our city, many were born here, all were commingled with us in our political, business and social life. They belonged to us because they were part of us.

"On that enticing morning when the skies were bright, the breezes fragrant with the perfumes of the forest wood, the dimpled lake blushing in the caressing sunlight; when all nature with inviting smile seemed to say 'Come and know me better,' with light hearts and merry laughter they left us, seeking rest from the anxiety and weariness of the week's toil."

Hall painted a word picture of the morning of the fateful excursion and the joy experienced by the passengers on the *Sea Wing*. But as everyone in the audience that day knew, that portrait was only part of the day, and he went on to illustrate a much different side of nature, the side that led to death and sadness.

> *The darkness deepened. It was such darkness as incessant lightning sometimes makes visible. The black-greenish clouds were hurled and tumbled in fantastic masses, driving upon and piling over each other, closing the jagged rents, shutting out forever the twilight, the stars and the blue. The lashed and foaming waters like famished wolves howled and snarled for their prey. The winds gathering in intensity, at first a gale, culminated in the tornado's blast. Far out on the waves they heard the trees upon the storm-battered bluffs twist and snap like crackling whips of a hemlock fire. The rain came, and the hail, more pitiless than the rain. Great zigzag flashes of lightning, footlights to the tragedy upon the lake, disclosed every threatening danger, illuminated every horror, exposed the futility of all hopes of succor or escape.*
>
> *The tempest in its fury, all the battling forces of nature in hostile combination were hurled against them. It was a night of terror, of despair, of death.*

Five thousand people attended a memorial service held in Red Wing on July 25, 1890. *Courtesy of the Goodhue County Historical Society.*

This memorial to the victims of the *Sea Wing* wreck is in Levee Park in Red Wing, which was the home of seventy-seven of the victims. *Photo by Steve Gardiner.*

Hall understood that the citizens of Red Wing and of the surrounding communities were asking why such a tragedy had happened. He acknowledged that the forces of nature are sometimes beyond our understanding, that we are often faced with the unknown. But he added that he believed the disaster of the *Sea Wing* had in it a lesson for everyone concerned.

He said many people get caught in a frenzy of accumulating more money, in the "petty selfishness" of business, and have neglected some of the more important things in life.

When news of the tragedy reached the communities, Hall said it "touched a responsive chord in every heart. It awakened a broader philanthropy, a more profound sympathy for the suffering, a deeper regret for those lost, a higher and better manhood than you or I have ever seen or may ever again see in any community. Everywhere and in every bosom there was a burning desire to lend a helping hand, to offer consolation to the distressed."

He said that in those moments, the good of mankind became our business.

3

MEMORIES AND MEMORIALS

In the storm that rolled his boat, Captain David Wethern lost both his wife and son Perley. His son Roy was saved. In addition to his family losses, Wethern received much criticism, both personally and in the media, for his actions on the evening of July 13. One report in the *Winona Daily News* said that he had been arrested on July 15 and was in jail in Ellsworth after friends requested he be taken in for his own protection, having received threats from friends of victims of the disaster.

On July 15, the *St. Paul Pioneer Press* ran an editorial that pointed an accusing finger at Wethern. "The deaths at Lake Gervais from a local wind storm, sad as they were, are not to be compared in horror with the tragedy on Lake Pepin. And this latter is clearly attributable to human recklessness, and disregard of the plainest lessons of the past."

Wethern felt the need to respond, so on July 17, he and ship's clerk E.M. Niles released their version of the events to newspapers in the form of a letter to the editor.

"Having heard so many reports of the wreck of the steamer Sea Wing that are incorrect, and thinking that a report from the captain and clerk of the boat, who were on her during it all, would be acceptable to you, we send a report of the trip exactly as it was, as we have seen no report that is exactly correct," they wrote in the *Winona Daily Herald*.

"The steamer Sea Wing had been recently inspected and found to be in good condition, and with barge she had in company, was allowed 250 passengers."

Captain David Wethern with his wife, Nellie Boyes Wethern, and sons Perley (*left*) and Roy. *Courtesy of the Goodhue County Historical Society.*

They listed the crew, which included, in addition to the two of them, M.L. Sparks, mate; Will Sparks, engineer; as well as crewmen Hank Hope, Will Niles, Harry Niles, West Willie, Charles Neal and Warren Spark. "There were on the boat and barge 200 floats, 187 cork and tule preservers and seven good skiffs with twenty-eight oars," they wrote.

The boat left Diamond Bluff at 7:40 a.m. with eleven passengers, Trenton at 8:30 with twenty-two more and Red Wing at 10:00 with 114 from that point; total, 147 passengers.

As the boat was about to return from Lake City there were two ladies from the steamer Wanderer and eight men from the steamer Undine who wished to take passage to Red Wing on the steamer Sea Wing. These with about ten more who were residents of Lake City and who wanted to go to Red Wing, came aboard; thus the list would have been about 175, but some few who came down on the excursion failed to get back before the boat left Lake City, hence the number of passengers was under 175. The boat left Lake City at eight o'clock, and proceeded up the lake about five miles. When the storm struck us the boat was completely and instantly overturned. Capt. Wethern was at the wheel and did all in his power to keep the boat headed into the wind and remained in the pilot house until completely submerged, then broke through the side and succeeded in reaching shore. The engineer stood at his post until the water filled the engine room, then made his escape. When the boat upset there was no water in her hull and nothing but the force of the wind upset her. The barge was not cut loose until the steamer capsized and then only to save it from being swamped also.

The boat was built at Diamond Bluff and was only three years old and was all built new throughout, machinery and all. The boat's tonnage was 109.55 tons. The crew were all able men and understood their business. No liquors were on board and none of the crew drank a drop that day, and more, none of the crew were drinking men. When the boat left Lake City the storm seemed to have passed, and the crew deemed it safe to start. The passengers also wanted to go, and so the boat started out on her return trip. The life preservers were such as the inspector ordered, and were all in good condition. The boat was to start back at five o'clock, but most of the number from Red Wing wished to remain until after the dress parade at seven. Hence the boat delayed until eight o'clock before starting.

Signed D.N. Wethern, Captain and E.M. Niles, Clerk

STORM WARNING

Inspectors in St. Paul called Wethern in for a hearing, and they pulled his pilot's license for "starting out in the face of a rising and threatening storm and yielding to the clamors of his passengers who were not supposed to know the dangers of navigation as well as he."

Local inspectors George B. Knapp and Charles S. Yeager submitted their report on August 22, 1890, to Supervising Inspector John D. Sloane. They reported in the *Minneapolis Tribune* that "there was every evidence of an approaching storm, although the witnesses in behalf of the steamer claim that it could not be seen from where she lay behind the Lake City point."

They recounted the wind blowing up the lake, then the sudden change and the squall that struck the *Sea Wing*. They also noted that the *Sea Wing*, at the time of the accident, was carrying about thirty more passengers than its certificate allowed and that the crew at the time was not sufficient.

They listed several sections of the Revised Statutes that Wethern and his crew violated and found him guilty of unskillfulness.

"Unskillfulness, by starting out as he did in the face of an approaching storm. Also after he had started out, by not running the Minnesota shore where there are good harbors every mile or so instead of up the center of the lake," they stated. "We, therefore, this day revoke his license as master and pilot, and report the case to the United States."

Two weeks after the accident, the *Netta Durant* hauled both the *Sea Wing* and the *Jim Grant* back to Diamond Bluff. The *Sea Wing* was rebuilt and operated out of St. Paul until about 1900, when its engines were moved into a towboat and part of the pilothouse became a henhouse. Several items from the boat were added to the collection at the Goodhue County Historical Society in Red Wing.

Thirty-six years after the wreck, Wethern, at age seventy-two, spoke with the *St. Paul Pioneer Press* about the events of July 13, 1890. At the time, Wethern was living in Prescott, Wisconsin, sharing a home with his son Roy, who was working on government steamboats as a captain, pilot or chief engineer.

"The Sea Wing tragedy might have broken some men," reported the *Pioneer Press.*

The *Sea Wing* was eventually towed to Diamond Bluff, Wisconsin, for restoration. *Courtesy of the Goodhue County Historical Society.*

> *Captain Wethern lost his wife and younger son; he himself faced death after the manner that often turns men's hair white; and he came through facing the condemnation that invariably falls on some one when an accident occurs. He was assailed in the press; he was hauled before the steamboat inspectors, and suspension of his pilot's license was ordered, and he suffered from hearing versions of the disaster that he knew to be untrue. But Captain Wethern had friends who stood by him; friends who accepted his account of the accident and held him to be the victim of circumstances rather than a blunderer as some others were charging.*

There were so many variables that could have turned out differently. The storm could have been a short time earlier or later. The *Sea Wing* could have been angled one direction or the other and faced a less direct hit from the straight-line wind. And the *Pioneer Press* even noted that if the events had been just slightly different and Wethern had been able to get the *Sea Wing* to a port, he may have even been hailed as a hero. "How many men similarly have become heroes—by the skin of their teeth!"

Wethern's license was removed, but it was reinstated in three years. He restored the *Sea Wing* and ran it on the river for more than a decade until he retired.

The *Pioneer Press* asked Wethern about the storm, and he recounted that he had been in the pilothouse alone. He had just passed another boat, whose crew made no mention of the storm. Wethern judged that the storm was not much to worry about, and he even noted that his son Roy, age eleven, had been standing near the rail in front of the cabin. The captain said he would have sent him inside if he suspected the storm would be bad. His wife had put son Perley to bed and was sitting in a rocking chair outside the door.

Wethern said that he nosed the boat out into Lake Pepin because he wanted to be out far enough to go around Point au Sable. He estimated that they were a quarter of a mile off Central Point when the winds hit. "Then the tornado came sweeping upon us, all in a moment," Wethern said. "The Sea Wing, with the lines holding it to the barge cut, was swept away from the barge and overturned in a flash."

Wethern said that a crew member cut the line between the *Sea Wing* and the *Jim Grant*. "He did it without order," Wethern said in the *Pioneer Press*. "Neither was an order issued by me, as some reports said, that all women and children should go from the barge into the cabins of the steamer. Nor did any one lock the cabin doors. I believe thoroughly that the wind would have driven us ashore, and we would have been safe if the barge had not been cut loose. The barge was driven ashore, and everyone aboard it was saved."

Wethern related his story that after the *Sea Wing* overturned, he pushed against the window and escaped under water. He surfaced several feet from the overturned boat and grabbed a plank but soon let go of it and climbed onto the bottom of the boat, as others had. He couldn't see who was with him, the night being too dark, so he immediately began asking about his wife and sons. He also said that while he and the others were clinging to the boat, large hailstones fell on them.

"The hail doubtless stunned and caused the death of many of those who were clinging to the hull of the steamer or to other articles or were swimming to the shore," he said. "When the bodies of Roderick Mero and his son Austin were recovered, I remember, deep bruises were found on their heads, evidently inflicted by hail stones. Both were good swimmers, and they had been seen holding to a plank, with every probability of reaching shore safely."

Wethern held onto the boat for several minutes, then decided to let go and swim ashore. When he arrived, he staggered, then found himself too exhausted to walk. He recounted that Ed Hall, who had arrived on shore earlier, saw him and helped him.

"The storm had subsided within a few minutes after the steamer capsized, and rescues began as soon as the skiffs could be manned and launched by those who had responded to the first calls for help," Wethern said. "My son, Roy, was among those saved. When the steamer capsized, he was thrown clear of the hull, and was pulled out of the water by a man who climbed upon the boat's bottom."

Wethern had built the *Sea Wing* three years before the accident. He assured the *Pioneer Press* that it was as strong as any boat on the river at the time and that he had met every safety requirement of the law.

WETHERN CONTINUED LIVING IN Diamond Bluff and running his general store for several years before moving to Prescott, Wisconsin. He married Josephine Wheeler of Prescott in 1905. He passed away in April 1929 at the age of seventy-five and is buried in the Diamond Bluff cemetery.

CASPER "CAP" HAUSTEIN HAD gone to church Sunday morning, and he noticed that several people seemed impatient with Father Gaughn's lengthy Mass. When he heard the whistle of the *Sea Wing*, he knew why. As the Mass ended, many people headed to the river, and Cap followed.

"I had not intended to go, but it seemed so interesting that I yielded to temptation and climbed aboard with hundreds of others," he told the *Red Wing Daily Republican* thirty-nine years after the wreck. "I don't believe Henry Rehder's old string band ever made a bunch step livelier than this joyous crowd did to the strains of their music."

Cap attended the ceremonies at Camp Lakeview with the rest, and as he was leaving, he saw several old-school companions and stopped to have a drink with them, noting that there was plenty of the "amber fluid" available and that it was "free of charge."

By the time Cap reached the boat landing at the end of Washington Street, the *Sea Wing* had departed.

"Grabbing a lantern, I ran down to the edge of the dock and waved for the boat to come back because there were three or four bus loads left behind," Cap said. "But the captain did not heed my signals. Had the boat turned back then, it would not have been able to get started again before the storm hit."

When the storm started, Cap and a few others took shelter in the candy store, listening to the rain and hail pounding on the awnings and tin roofs of the buildings. When the storm ended, Cap and his friend Will Becker decided to head out along the shore of the lake, worried about friends and family who were on the *Sea Wing*.

"We progressed by flashes of lightning," Cap said. "Through a bunch of bull rushes we ran and stumbled on a young man who was very much excited. We asked him if he knew anything of the Sea Wing, and he said he had swum ashore from it and that most of the women and children were drowned."

E.M. Schenach, who played bass viol on the *Sea Wing*, was the last known survivor of the wreck, passing away in 1962 at the age of ninety-six. *Courtesy of the Goodhue County Historical Society.*

The pair continued along the shore until they saw the barge. They picked up pieces of wreckage, piled them up and made a bonfire to alert people.

"No sooner was the blaze started when a skiff came to shore with two men and a body which they had taken from the boat. It was my cousin, Annie Staiger," Cap said. They attempted to resuscitate her, but the attempts failed, and not long after, another skiff pulled up with the body of Annie's sister Francis Staiger.

When the National Guard arrived, Will and Cap helped them with the bodies through the night. Cap then took the train back to Red Wing, arriving there about six o'clock in the morning.

"The people were all excited and wanted to know something about their loved ones," Cap said. "They rushed upon me, and I had to take the middle of the street to get to my home which was on East Seventh Street. Arriving home, mother met me with a stick because I had not told her I was going and the strain had made her nearly distracted. I retreated until I got my breath and was able to give an explanation."

Cap then borrowed a horse and wagon and rode into the country to deliver news to several people who had lost family members in the tragedy.

A modern look at the view Captain Wethern and passengers would have had coming around Central Point (*left foreground*) and heading toward Maiden Rock (*right background*). *Photo by Steve Gardiner.*

The second point that Captain Wethern wanted to circle around is Point au Sable, or Sandpoint, shown extending well into the lake. Several boats are beached on the point. The bluff rising behind is the upper level of Frontenac State Park. *Photo by Steve Gardiner.*

Looking south from approximately the point where the *Sea Wing* tipped, Central Point is visible in front of the sailboat on the right. The sailboat on the left is closer to Lake City, showing the distance that help from Lake City had to travel to reach the capsized *Sea Wing* and the *Jim Grant*, which drifted to Central Point. *Photo by Steve Gardiner.*

HAILSTONES

Forty years after the *Sea Wing* disaster, Milt Davis, writing in the *Minneapolis Tribune*, tried to understand the impact that the event, one of the worst disasters in state history, had on Minnesota.

"There were striking circumstances contributing to make the capsizing of the Sea Wing memorable," Davis wrote.

> *There was, to begin with, the heavy loss of life. There was the grim contrast between the lightheartedness of the excursionists and the terror of the catastrophe suddenly blown upon them. There was the helplessness of the victims to save themselves. There were fateful turns of decision— anxious glances at approaching clouds, hesitancy over putting off from shore, reckless resolution, the final start—which entailed so much of woe. And there were deeds of heroism, to relieve somewhat, the drab tale.*

The storm rolled the boat over, but it did not quit then. It took the struggling victims who were hanging on to the overturned boat or floating debris and pelted them with "great hailstones, missiles that stunned them and tore many of them from pieces of wreckage they had frantically grasped."

Davis noted that by 1930, the steamboat days were over on the Mississippi River, their brief but significant history largely forgotten, except for the events surrounding the *Sea Wing* disaster.

For the article, Davis interviewed Harry Mabey, the young boy who had escaped the barge and ran into Lake City to sound the alarm for help. Mabey said that when he and his friends boarded the *Sea Wing* for the return trip, one friend, Charley Sewell, did not like a dark cloud on the horizon and said he would not go. Mabey said Sewell jumped over the side and swam four hundred feet to shore.

The other boys went inside the cabin but soon came back out. There were some life preservers on deck, and each boy grabbed one just moments before the *Sea Wing* capsized.

"As the boat rolled over, everybody on our side slid down," Mabey remembered. "We made a jump for the barge. One of the boys went through the canopy top, one struck a post and rolled off, while I myself missed the barge entirely. But as I came up out of the water, I grabbed its side and managed to climb aboard the barge."

The barge was drifting toward Central Point. In the dark, Mabey couldn't tell where he was, but as the barge moved close to the shore, he and others jumped. Another boy landed on Mabey, and they scrambled up onto the shore. It was there that Mabey experienced the hailstorm.

"The stones were big and they pelted us unmercifully," he said. "I crawled up onto the beach to a bunch of little bushes and took my life preserver and put it over my head to keep the hailstones off."

The hail ended quickly, and Mabey headed for Lake City, about two miles away. He arrived there and went to the fire hall and rang the bell. The wind had died down by then, so Mabey and Theed Minder jumped in a skiff and rowed back to Central Point.

"The Sea Wing had drifted around the point, out of the wind," Mabey explained, "and was lying broadside out in about twenty-five feet of water. We reached the boat, coming in on the windward side. We backed up very carefully and took eighteen persons off in three loads. These persons had clung to the boat as she rolled over three or four times."

The final load of people was too much for the skiff, and the boat sank. Fortunately, it was in three feet of water, so all aboard could easily walk ashore.

FOR THE *TRIBUNE* ARTICLE, Davis also talked to another survivor, Samuel Haskell Purdy, who said he had been so upset that he could not stay indoors during a storm for years after the accident.

Purdy and his brother William had decided to take a train back to Red Wing instead of the *Sea Wing*, but when they got to the station, the train had already departed. They returned and boarded the *Sea Wing*. Not long after the vessel departed Lake City, the wind hit.

"For an instant the lake was clear, swept clean of waves," Purdy said. "Then the wind scooped up the water and tossed it high into the air. The boat careened, capsized completely, turned bottom-side up."

At that moment, Purdy and his brother had been standing at the rail in front of the cabin. As the boat flipped, Purdy said he looked at the cabin and saw the women and girls inside. He said he had never forgotten that image.

The Purdy brothers held onto the rail as the boat went over. When the storm stopped, they swam ashore and took a train home the next day.

"THERE ARE NOT TOO many residents of this area who can remember the Sea Wing disaster," wrote the *Winona Daily News* in a 1956 retelling of the tragedy. "But the frequent recounting of this tragedy should leave its impress behind. What happened to the Sea Wing can happen to other people who take chances with the weather when storms threaten. Lake Pepin and the Mississippi River, so benign in appearance under the summer sun, are destructive giants when high winds stir their wrath. Sensible people take no chances on these waters—at any time of the year."

The day after the *Sea Wing* wreck, the *Red Wing Republican* ran a long article about the event, calling it the "most terrible catastrophe." The article ended with a list of all those who survived—and those who did not.

"The majority, in fact, nearly all of these were residents of this city and the irreparable loss, therefore, comes all the heavier to us," the *Republican* stated. "It has cast a gloom over our city that time cannot dispel wholly, for a calamity of this kind can never be forgotten."

Businesses closed. Flags flew at half-mast across the city. People walked through the streets in disbelief, talking to each other, consoling each other and wondering how they would continue after such a huge disaster had befallen their community.

A composite photo showing the victims of the *Sea Wing* tragedy. *Courtesy of the Goodhue County Historical Society.*

On Friday, July 18, the *Red Wing Daily Republican* summed up the tragic week: "But little remains to be said with reference to the Sunday disaster. The dead have all been buried, and business is slowly resuming its normal condition after a period of almost complete paralysis."

Eventually, Red Wing was able to return to daily living. The *Sea Wing* disaster is a powerful part of local history and is forever marked on a memorial in Levee Park.

✦In Memoriam.✦

Orrin Oskey,
Minnie Fisher,
Frederick Seavers,
Ida Seavers,
Hattie Scherf,
Mrs. F. Scherf,
Martin Scherf.
Herman Hempftling,
Mrs. Herman Hempftling,
Mrs. F. Hempftling.
Fred E. Hempftling,
Lizzie Hempftling,
Emma Nelson,
Melissa A. Harrison,
George Nelson,
Phœbe Bearson,
Annie Schneider,
Mrs. O. Nelson,
Bertha Winter,
Mary Olson,
Mabel Holton,
John Strope,
Nettie Palmer,
John Ingebritson,
Theodor Horwedel,
John Behrens.
Mrs. John Behrens,
Julia Persig,
Annie Persig,
Mrs. Johanna Humpert,
Peter Olson,
Aggie Palmer,
Mary Skoglund.
Henry Newton,
Joseph Carlson,
Eliza J. Crawford,
Mrs. D. N. Wethern,
Perley Wethern,
James Wilson,
Annie Staiger,
Frances Staiger,
Ira Fulton,
Rosa Rehder,
Henry Rehder,
F. J. Christ,
Louis Brenn,
Charles Peterson,
Edward Ingebritson,
William Jorgenson,

Rikka Veiths,
Knute Peterson,
Charles Brown,
Henry Steffenson,
Mrs. E. Larson,
Thomas Leeson,
Kate Dailey,
Charles Dinslage,
Fred Hattemer,
George Hartman,
John Schoeffler,
Mrs. J. Schoeffler,
John Schoeffler, Jr.,
Frederick Schoeffler,
Mrs. Sophia Schulenberg,
Henry Schulenberg,
Mamie Schulenberg,
Randine Olson,
William Adams,
Ella Adams,
John Adams,
Mamie Adams,
Mattie Flinn,
Cord Johnson,
Mrs. Merritt Green,
Ida Green,
R. L. Mero,
Austin Mero,
Myrtle Mero,
Mrs. Creemer,
Leon Creemer,
Millie Niles,
Flora Smith.
A. O. Anderson,
Martin O'Shaughnessy,
Edith Way,
Edna Way,
Gustaf L. Lillyblad,
Mrs. W. S. Blaker,
Cena Blaker,
Dell W. Blaker,
Peter Gerken,
Mrs. Peter Gerken,
Henry Gerken,
Amandus Gerken,
George Gerken,
Alvina H. Gerken,
Emil J. Gerken,
Kate Burkard,

A list of those who perished during the *Sea Wing* disaster. *Courtesy of the Goodhue County Historical Society.*

The Wreck of the *Sea Wing* (1890)

When Father Louis Hennepin first placed Lake Pepin on his 1683 map of the area, he referred to Lake Pepin as Lac des Pleurs, or Lake of the Tears. While the name did not stick, it certainly seemed appropriate after the tragic events of July 13, 1890.

PART II

THE ARMISTICE DAY BLIZZARD (1940)

4

DID NOT GET HOME

Duck hunting had been a little slow in the fall of 1940. That year, November 11, Armistice Day—renamed Veteran's Day in 1954—fell on a Monday, so hunters were out taking advantage of a three-day weekend and hoping to improve their luck.

The weather had been good all weekend, and some hunters reported listening to the Gophers' football game on Saturday in their shirtsleeves. The long weekend was a hunter's dream, and many had made plans to get outside and enjoy it.

The morning was mild. Hunters from Prairie Island to Winona headed out to islands in the Mississippi River and occupied their favorite blinds. Wood decoys floated in the waters in front of them as the hunters waited for ducks to fly in.

Owen Redman and Arnold Vogel from Red Wing decided they would work until noon, then go hunting after lunch. They showed up at Colvill Park at 1:00 p.m. and found that the weather was quickly changing.

"It was starting to spit snow," Redman said in a 1990 article in the *Republican Eagle*. "We got down to the river, and we could see the whitecaps. We looked at each other. Not a word was spoken. We turned around and went back to work."

They were lucky. By that time, scores of other hunters were already on islands. A light rain had turned to snow, and the winds suddenly increased to fifty miles per hour. The temperature dropped from the forties to ten degrees. Many hunters left quickly and made their way back to their homes, but others, thinking the storm would pass, remained in their blinds.

An aerial view of the Mississippi River bottomland near Winona, where several hunters were caught during the blizzard. *Courtesy of the Winona County Historical Society.*

Dan Kukowski from Winona had left home that morning and rode his bicycle across the bridge to a spot on the Wisconsin side, where he and some other hunters had locked their boats along the shore. He paddled his canoe to an island, where he found other hunters.

As the winds changed, the hunters were excited, because the ducks were flocking in. The shooting was good. "We thought the ducks would come, so we stayed," Kukowski recalled in a 1985 issue of the *Minnesota Volunteer*. "And sure enough, they came in. Well, it started to get so windy that when you shot a duck the wind carried it a couple of blocks away."

He said the willow trees were lying flat because of the wind. As the temperature quickly dropped, hunters were looking around for any dry branches for firewood. Many were forced to burn their wood decoys to keep warm. Kukowski said many hunters huddled together and others hid under overturned boats for protection. The scene was rapidly turning tragic.

"I saw one friend sitting against a tree," Kukowski said. "He was frozen to death. I had seen him that morning. He told me he was going hunting and fishing both, because the weather was so nice."

Like many others, Kukowski was dressed in light clothing. With the storm worsening, he felt he would freeze if he stayed on the island, so, at 4:30 p.m., he got in his canoe and headed for shore. The river was choppy, and big waves tossed his canoe around.

"It took about an hour," he said. "You couldn't see over the waves. That's how big they were. It was the only time I was ever scared on the river. I thought I was going to die."

Another friend on shore recognized Kukowski's boat bouncing around in the waves and watched him struggle. Kukowski finally reached shore far down from where he had originally crossed, and his friend took him home.

ICY OARS

Near Prairie Island, north of Red Wing, the scene was similar. Abe Kuhns, who lived in a farmhouse on Sturgeon Lake, had been hunting that day with a man named Brestkamp from St. Paul, according to an article in the *Red Wing Daily Republican*. The pair had stayed out well into the storm, but as night approached, they headed for home. As Kuhns rowed along the island, he saw five men with a gasoline-powered boat. They said they intended to stay, but Kuhns persuaded them to leave. They later reported that it took them five hours to travel one mile to safety.

"The wind was now a gale, a demon that howled in astonishment at the magnitude of its destructiveness," reported the *Daily Republican*. "It roared across the lake out of the north, ripping the whitecaps from the six-foot waves and hurling them thirty feet up on to shore in frozen crystals. It reached out icy hands towards straggling hunters, now frantic with the knowledge of their peril; fighting a grim fight with death by the elements."

In one account, Kuhns continued rowing along the island and came across three more stranded hunters. They were, as a *Daily Republican* editorial reported, "out there in the open, a prey to the full force of the storm. Their frail duck boat laid on shore. It couldn't have lasted a minute in the teeth of that gale that sped down the slough at the speed of a freight train. One of the men appeared to be in a bad way."

The ailing hunter got into Kuhns's boat, and he again pulled against the oars. The distance was not far, and Kuhns knew the country well, having hunted and fished there all his life, but the wind and waves made the crossing difficult and dangerous. When he reached the shore, Brestkamp and the hunter got out of the boat, and Kuhns rowed back to the island to get the other hunters and bring them back to shore.

"The oarsman kept on rowing," noted the *Daily Republican*. "Inch by inch, foot by foot, into the darkness and snow and biting temperatures, with his soaked clothes and aching muscles, he fought across that narrow strip of water where death lashed its whitecapped horsemen."

The editorial stated that Kuhns, his oars and his boat were coated in a thick layer of ice, making it even more difficult to row. The weight of the bodies and the ice caused the boat to sink deeper into the cold water. In spite of the struggle, Kuhns was able to return the two other hunters to the shore and to safety and warmth.

Other accounts of Kuhns's exploits were published over the ensuing days. Five days after the storm, the *Red Wing Daily Republican* reported that Kuhns's brother Tony had told him about six hunters who had taken boats to a small island separating Sturgeon Lake from the Mississippi River. Hearing that, Kuhns "went directly to the landing and bailed out a boat."

> *He set out alone across the freezing whitecaps. It was not luck alone that let him row through the hidden stumps unscathed, but years of experience and a natural skill. After he had rescued the first two hunters, he realized that his boat was not large enough to take more than two passengers at a time, so Abe made two more trips, carrying two thankful hunters across to Tony's warm house with each crossing. When the last man had been rescued, Abe went home to finish his chores. Before he went out to the barn, though, he stopped into his own house and thawed out his hands and his face, which had been frozen quite badly.*

"The real hero of the area was Abe Kuhns," said Owen Redman in a 1990 *Red Wing Republican Eagle* article. "He rowed across Sturgeon Lake in a flat-bottomed boat. He made six trips across. How he made one is beyond me."

The number of hunters involved and the number of trips made by Kuhns vary in the reports, but it is consistent that he set out alone and was able to rescue stranded hunters who likely would have perished if left to the elements through the night.

According to a *Daily Republican Eagle* article on the first anniversary of the Armistice Day Blizzard, Dr. Fred Andersen and several of Kuhns's friends

Abe Kuhns was able to make several dangerous trips out on the river in a rowboat to rescue duck hunters from islands near Red Wing. *Courtesy of the Goodhue County Historical Society.*

determined to nominate him for a Carnegie Medal for his heroism. They sent paperwork to the Carnegie Hero Fund commission in Pittsburgh, and the commission, after requesting additional information, sent Irwin Urling, one of its agents, to investigate. Urling submitted his report to the commission, and at the next meeting, it evaluated the nomination.

Andersen received a letter signed by C.B. Ebersol, manager of the fund, stated that "the case of Abraham R. Kuhns has been considered by the commission, and it has been decided that it is not within the scope of the Fund."

"The fact that Abe Kuhns will not get a medal, or a grant of money, makes him no less a hero," stated the *Daily Republican Eagle*. "There was no thought of reward in his mind when he risked his life in the Armistice day blizzard. He was perfectly aware of the risk he was taking, but that did not cause him to hesitate."

Though he did not receive the Carnegie Medal, Kuhns was locally deemed a hero and did receive statewide recognition.

In 1943, the *Winona Republican-Herald* reported that Kuhns had been awarded a citation for heroism from the Minnesota Safety Council, noting that "Kuhn [sic], during the height of the 1940 Armistice day blizzard, made three trips across Truttman slough to rescue six hunters marooned on an island and apparently doomed to death."

The *Daily Republican Eagle* editorial described Kuhns as having "rugged features, stamped with character and weather beaten with a life spent outdoors."

According to the piece, Kuhns was a little embarrassed by the attention. He said, "I didn't do it for the glory. Those men needed savin' and I just went out and saved 'em."

FREEZING TEMPERATURES

Downriver from Prairie Island, others were at work trying to help stranded hunters. Owen Redman and Arnold Vogel, who had earlier in the day returned to work rather than go out on the river in the building storm, boarded a cruiser along with a *Minnesota Star* photographer, according to a 1990 article in the *Red Wing Republican Eagle*.

"The biggest job fell to Vogel, because he had to pilot the boat safely between wing dams beneath the water surface. In the summer, buoys marked

This cruiser boat was involved in the rescue of several hunters from islands and later for the recovery of hunters who died during the 1940 Armistice Day Blizzard. *Courtesy of the Goodhue County Historical Society.*

the dams of rock piles, but the Army Corps of Engineers pulled the buoys in the autumn. Snow also limited the vision."

Vogel was eighty-six in 1990 when he told the *Republican Eagle* that the spray from the bow of the boat was icing the windshield, forcing him to leave the windshield open and exposing himself to the spray.

"We went to shore eight or ten times," Vogel said. "We looked for footprints, but never saw any. We'd shoot a gun in the air, but nobody answered our call."

Without any success, they decided to turn around and went upstream to Lock and Dam 3, where the lockmaster told them that other boaters had reported two hunters farther upriver.

Vogel and Redman found a ladder and a lantern on a small island at Miley's Run, across the river from Diamond Bluff, Wisconsin. They landed and soon found the two men frozen to death.

Redman explained that the river was knee-deep off one end of the island, but nine feet deep at the other end. Apparently, the men had become confused in the chaos of the storm and had walked off the wrong end. "These men had waded out," Redman said. "They were soaked to their armpits."

With the help of Art Halvorson, Ray DuBois and Andy Anderson, the crew was able to carry the two bodies to the shoreline, where they found a dilapidated rowboat crusted in ice. They placed the bodies in the rowboat and used it to transfer the bodies to the cruiser, well aware of the precarious situation for all involved.

According to the *Republican Eagle*, Coroner Russell F. Edstrom and Deputy Sheriff Paul Zillgitt left for the scene and later identified the two bodies as Carl Iverson, forty-one, and Melville Roberts, forty-two, both of St. Paul. That's when Redman realized that Roberts was his cousin.

"We didn't think what we did was important compared to what other people did," Redman told the *Republican Eagle*. "The story was the same all along, up and down the river."

TWO DAYS AFTER THE Armistice Day storm, the *Daily Republican* ran another story about Roberts and Iverson. They had stopped at the home of Vendle Hanson at Prairie Island near North Lake. The pair had a letter from a friend of Hanson's stating that they had permission to use a boat the friend had stored there for the hunting season.

After visiting with Hanson, the two hunters set out for Miley's Run, a narrow channel that connects Chain Lake, by then part of the dam pool,

Saturday November 10, 1990 R.W. Rep. Eag.

Armistice Day storm left death, heroes

Several died at Red Wing 50 years ago

By Anne Jacobson
STAFF WRITER

Owen Redman and Arnold Vogel would have been heroes. But the blizzard was too quick and too severe.

Fifty years ago, the raging Armistice Day storm swept through the Midwest, turning a duck hunters' paradise into a wasteland. The blizzard left 59 Minnesotans dead and thousands stranded.

The weekend began with 50-degree weather. Golden Gopher fans in short sleeves packed the football stadium. Hunters carrying only rain gear and guns hurried to reach their duck blinds. Nov. 11 fell on a Monday and people took advantage of the three-day weekend.

Fishing canceled

Redman, 68, of Red Wing worked at the local creamery. He and his hunting partner, Allen Hall, decided they would head about noon for Dead Slough Lake across from Colvill Park. It was raining and ducks generally follow a change in the weather, he said. But in a blink of an eye, warm rain turned to sleet. With the change in the weather, Redman and Hall changed their minds.

"I went home from work at 12 p.m. for lunch. It was starting to spit snow," Redman recalled. "We got down to the river and we could see the whitecaps. We looked at each other. Not a word was spoken. We turned around and went back to work."

Other hunters didn't heed the weather. The temperature dropped from 40 to 10 degrees. Afterward, people reported stories of hordes of ducks flying backward in attempts to go against the wind. Choppy waves and blinding snow stranded men on islands in the Mississippi around Red Wing and Prairie Island.

No local hunters died because they knew where to seek shelter or knew how to survive in a storm, Redman said. Twin Cities hunters, however, weren't as knowledgeable. Five or six perished. The same number survived because of one late Prairie Island man.

"The real hero of the area was Abe Kuhns. He rowed across Sturgeon Lake in a flat-bottom boat. He made six trips across. How he made one is beyond me. The lake was filled with stumps below the surface," Redman said.

To the rescue

On the morning of Nov. 12, the Goodhue County Sheriff's Office estimated 40 to 50 men still missing. The storm had knocked out telephone lines and closed roads, but deputies knew people were stranded because of vacant cars and empty boat trailers.

Turn to BLIZZARD, page 12

Rescuers at Miley's Cut, north of Prairie Island, didn't reach two St. Paul hunters in time. In front from left, Arnold Vogel and Art Halvorson grip the frozen coat of Melville Roberts. Ray DuBois and Andy Anderson are behind. — photos courtesy of the Goodhue County Historical Society

Local searchers load the bodies of Melville Roberts and Cal Iverson, both of St. Paul, into a cruiser on the Mississippi River. The two men perished in the 1940 Armistice Day storm.

A *Red Wing Republican Eagle* story from 1990 showed photos of rescuers carrying the body of Melville Roberts of St. Paul, a duck hunter who died in the blizzard, and the scene of the bodies of Roberts and Cal Iverson being loaded onto a boat. *Courtesy of the Goodhue County Historical Society.*

with the Mississippi River, a distance of about one mile from the Hanson farm. As the rain turned to sleet and then snow, Hanson realized that the hunters would have a very difficult time getting back, but he determined it would be suicide to set out in a boat in the dark with all the tree stumps in the dam pool. He left his door unlocked and lights on in case the hunters made it back and needed a place to stay.

On Tuesday morning, Hanson set out walking on a thin layer of ice along a road that was now underwater. "One hour after he had left home, Hanson discovered some tracks near the water's edge and followed them, finding Roberts, one of the hunters, standing near the body of his companion, Iverson, which lay face down in the bushes," the *Daily Republican* reported.

Hanson said that Roberts was completely exhausted, but Hanson wanted to get him somewhere to give him some help. "I told him I'd take him home and warm him up," Hanson said, "and he said O.K., so we started out. We walked about a quarter of a mile, with him stumbling and grabbing on to tree trunks for support. Finally I saw that we were not making any headway, so I stopped and built a fire for him, then I gave him a drink of brandy to stimulate him some."

Hanson walked back to his house, arriving there just after noon. He called a neighbor, Jesse Samuelson, to help him, and the two of them left Hanson's house about 2:00 p.m. When they arrived at the spot where Hanson had built the fire, Roberts was on the ground near the fire, but the fire had gone cold. He had not added any wood during the time Hanson was gone. They tried to give Roberts coffee, but he wasn't able to swallow it.

"Hanson and Samuelson realized by this time that the exhausted Roberts would never reach the Hanson home on his own, so they made a stretcher from some saplings, and loaded him onto it," reported the *Daily Republican*. "They had carried him in this manner for one-half a mile when Roberts died. At this point, Earl Flynn, Bud Flynn, Richard Johnson, Ted Samuelson, and Fritz Brescamp, all neighbors, arrived to help, and they carried the body of Roberts back to where Iverson lay on Miley's Run. Then they marked the spot with a ladder, so it would be possible for a searching party to find the bodies from the river."

It was the ladder seen by the rescuers in the cruiser boat piloted by Arnold Vogel.

Hanson remembered that when he had first reached Roberts and Iverson, the wind was making so much noise that he did not hear a steamboat that passed by them until it was too far upriver. "If I had seen it in time, I would have hailed it, and had them take Roberts on to Hastings for medical care," Hanson said.

One other duck hunter was hunting near Roberts and Iverson. When the wind increased, Otto Schuman loaded his boat, yelling at Roberts and Iverson, warning them to head back. "They paid no attention," Schuman told the *Daily Republican*, "and I could hear them shooting yet at four o'clock when I got back to Hanson's."

Schuman said that when he got back to his car, his clothing was so stiff from the ice that he could not sit down with his coat on.

FARTHER DOWN THE RIVER, Hjalmer Hjermstad owned a cruiser called the *Malihini* that was built in 1937 by the Marblehead Boat Company of Biddleford, Maine. Hjermstad brought the boat to Red Wing. Late in the day on November 11, 1940, Hjermstad and Game Warden Phil Nordeen, Police Chief Eric Carlson and Dick Bird took the cruiser out to search several islands.

"Before the night was over, two stranded hunters on an island near the head of Lake Pepin were to owe their lives to this quartet," reported the *Daily Republican*.

JACK HIEBEL AND HANK Satrum were both barbers in Zumbrota. Although they ran competing businesses, they were friends and frequent hunting partners. As soon as the ducks were flying, the two would close their shops and head to Wabasha and the Mississippi River, often renting a boat from Joe Wilcox's dock.

"So that no one would squawk when I took off, I would put a sign on the door, 'Duck hunting with Jack,'" Satrum said in a 1991 article in the *Zumbrota News*. "Jack would put a sign on his door, 'Hunting with Hank.'"

On November 11, they went to Wabasha and got a boat. They set out and promptly got rained on. They were wet, but not cold, so they continued to hunt and had very good luck shooting birds. They decided to take a break and eat lunch and then move on to another island farther from shore. They realized they had left their lunches in their car, a 1936 Ford, so they went back to eat.

When they set out after lunch, the water was so rough that they had trouble even getting back to the first island. Then, in an instant, it was snowing hard. "I've never seen anything like it," Satrum said. "It was like a fog, and it was so fine that when you breathed, it would fill your mouth and nose."

They decided to return to shore. They knew a barber from Wabasha, and he had been hunting on the same island, but "he was one of the casualties they never found," Satrum said.

Satrum and Hiebel set out to drive back to Zumbrota. They had a habit of stopping in Lake City at the Blue Moon Cafe for a T-bone steak, but the weather forced them to continue driving directly to Zumbrota.

"Our wives didn't worry about us until we got home and told them about the conditions," Satrum told the *Zumbrota News*. "I don't know if we really realized how bad the weather was. I guess we are lucky that we got back at all. Many didn't."

WILLIS KRUGER WAS NEW on the job as a game warden when he was thrust into the fierceness of the Armistice Day Blizzard. He worked along the Mississippi River in Wabasha County and was intending to go out and check duck hunters' licenses that day. Instead, he ended up spending the day warning hunters to go home and then spent the next several days searching for and rescuing others. There is one telling comment in his field notes for November 11. "Did not get home."

5

STRANDED IN SNOW AND ICE

Many people did not get home that day. Mrs. Frank T. Dahlgren, a Sunday correspondent with the *Winona Daily News* in 1963, recalled how she and her husband had spent eight years working aboard Dr. Will Mayo's yacht, the *North Star*. He served as the engineer, and she was the chief stewardess. The boat's home port was Wabasha.

Their stint aboard the *North Star* had ended, so they settled on thirteen acres of land near Wabasha and were in the process of remodeling buildings and making a home for themselves there. They had a dock where they rented slips to houseboats and a few boats that they rented to hunters.

By 5:00 a.m. on November 11, Dahlgren had rented all her boats and the hunters had headed out. She had seen several hunters pass by her property, headed for the backwaters. She was disappointed that she could not go hunting that day, as she needed to monitor the dock to help boaters. She spent the morning fishing from the dock.

"About 10:30, a boat owner called from Rochester, worried about the family boat, the Gypsy Jan," Dahlgren wrote. "She said the barometer was dropping rapidly. She asked if I would start a fire in the boat so the water lines wouldn't freeze if it turned cold. I assured her that the weather in Wabasha was mild."

Not long after, her husband called her from St. Paul and said it was snowing there. It was blowing so hard that he and some others had formed a human chain to help a woman get into a building. He said he wouldn't be home that night.

"I looked upriver past the interstate bridge, and saw ducks flying downriver as fast as they could move," she wrote. "I watched several flocks go by and realized they were flying before a storm. By then the sky was becoming heavily overcast. It got worse by the minute, and the wind was rising."

Dahlgren changed her mind and gathered firewood to start a fire inside the *Gypsy Jan* and another in the potbellied stove in her house to warm a soup kettle in case cold hunters came in. She threw all the anchors of the remaining boats upstream to hold them solid and keep them from banging into each other.

By then it was four o'clock, and the sky was darkening. A couple of hunters returned, talking about their oars freezing in the oarlocks. Bill Swenson, a Rochester carpenter, and his guide, Jack Hughley, arrived. Dahlgren said they were so cold they could hardly talk. Swenson called his son in Rochester to have him drive over and pick him up, but his son said there was no way he could drive in the storm and would have to wait to drive over in the morning.

Her phone rang, and a man named William Webb said his son was on an island off Pugh's Point and wanted to know if anyone could help. Dahlgren told Webb that she had no authority to take anyone else's boat out. A short time later, Webb called back to say his son had made it to shore with the help of a man named Murray Braun, whose mother ran a farm near the point.

While Dahlgren was talking with Webb, she saw the headlights of two cars approaching in the storm. The first was the car of policeman Chuck Gilbert, and the second car carried two men from Hayward, Wisconsin, with news that they needed help rescuing seven men stranded on an island. When the cold moved in, these two men had taken thermos bottles and gone to Alma, Wisconsin, to fill them with hot coffee and bring them back to the other hunters. By the time they filled the bottles, they were unable to row back to the island to get the other men.

Gilbert asked Hughley to help. Hughley chose a boat called the *Lazy Daisy*, and Dahlgren gathered wood and started a fire in the heater. Then she and one of the hunters from Hayward climbed aboard with Hughley and Webb, and they set out after the seven stranded hunters.

"It was dark now, snowing hard and blowing," Dahlren explained. "Bill untied the bow line and I the stern line. Bill got on and Chuck and I pushed the bow out to get it away from the dock. I jumped on board. I was going along as I was responsible for letting the boat go without the owner's permission."

As they left the dock, Dahlgren watched the boat shed disappear in the darkness. She knew the river area well, but at that point, everything was black. Hughley asked her to watch for any lights at Pugh's Point.

"That is when I looked down river and saw nothing except black and white," she said. "Our searchlight pierced the darkness only about three feet, snow was piling past, absorbing the light. I strained my eyes for bonfires along shore and the light at Pugh's. I couldn't even see the shore."

The wind howled, and at one point, a gust lifted the small lifeboat off the back of the *Lazy Daisy* and hurled it into the night. The waves were high enough that, at times, the propeller was lifted out of the water and spun freely in the air until the stern dropped back into the water.

Then the motor stopped. Hughley said it was wrapped with weeds. They were close to a small island, and Webb managed to tie the boat to the island. Dahlgren offered to get into the water and clear the propeller, but Hughley said, "We aren't going any place or doing anything tonight."

They found some food and ate, then wrapped themselves in blankets and stood near the heater, rocking endlessly in the storm.

Just after midnight, the boat stopped rocking and Dahlgren looked outside to see what was happening. The *Lazy Daisy* was frozen in ice.

In the morning, Hughley cut a sapling about ten feet long and had the others hold on to it. He used another stick to test the thickness of the ice. They set out to cross a quarter of a mile of ice to reach the Wilcox farm.

Dahlgren wrote that Hughley "carried the heavy stick to tap the ice to find a safe passage. He held one end of the willow pole. I was about four feet behind him hanging onto the pole. George (the hunter from Hayward) was about three feet behind me, and Bill was at the other end of the pole. If Jack fell in, we were to stop in our tracks. I never did figure out what we would have done if he had. Thank goodness, I didn't have to."

The crossing was a delicate one. They stepped gently.

"We walked like we were stepping on eggs, slowly. No one said a word. I was so scared I don't believe I even shivered. I don't remember taking a breath. It was difficult to breath the cold, sharp, windy air."

When they reached the shore, Dahlgren looked back and could barely make out the shape of the *Lazy Daisy* with its bright orange deck paint covered in show and ice. They walked to the Joe Wilcox farm where they were able to eat and get warm. They also learned that the Wabasha barber, Herbert Juenemann, had drowned. His hunting partner had been able to swim to shore, and Juenemann's body had not been recovered.

Mrs. Wilcox also told them about a hunter from Rochester who had been trapped on the same island where the *Lazy Daisy* had spent the night. He had started a bonfire about three hundred yards from where the *Lazy Daisy* had been icebound and burned his boat, oars and decoys. He was rescued about one o'clock in the morning, but those aboard the *Lazy Daisy* had not seen him or the rescue boat, and no one on the rescue boat had seen the *Lazy Daisy*.

Dahlgren also learned that the seven men they had set out to rescue made it out. One of their group realized that the two men who went to get coffee were not going to make it back, so "he removed his clothes and swam to shore to get a boat," Dahlgren wrote. "He made six trips, taking one man off the island at a time. He swam, pushing the boat ahead of him." He ended up in a Menomonie hospital being treated for exposure.

In the days that followed, Dahlgren, though she had lived through the freezing night, suffered other problems.

When her husband arrived from St. Paul, he said he couldn't believe anyone would head out in a boat during that kind of a storm. A few days later, the *Lazy Daisy* was towed back to the dock. The owner was angry and let Dahlgren know it. Dahlgren said she listened for fifteen minutes, then spoke her own mind.

"Now, listen here, if we had rescued one hunter from the storm that night, we would be heroes, but because we got the boat stuck in the ice and shallow water, we are fools," she responded.

The night had been a major experience for Dahlgren and soon sent her in a new direction. "The storm, the abuse for help I had tried to give, the heartbreak, the loneliness—I couldn't stand it any longer, so I left the Mississippi, and in a few months found a new way of life: In the service of my country in World War II."

BLOWING SNOW

In a 1977 reflection on the blizzard in the *Republican Eagle*, Frank Callister noted that he had tuned his radio to listen to the final high school football game of the season between Rochester and Winona. It was a close game, and the results were not at all clear by halftime. At the start of the second half, snow was blowing outside Callister's window as he listened.

"I watched the wind and the snow join in a partnership that formed miniature drifts that crawled across the sidewalk," he wrote. "An hour earlier the snow would have melted as it reached the ground, but now the lawn was becoming covered with a dusty white coating. The radio announcer mentioned snow flurries. He acknowledged a sudden drop in temperature."

Callister said the radio announcer reported that the field was getting white and that it was getting harder to tell the numbers on the players' jerseys. He added that some of the crowd were leaving the stadium.

"These people didn't come prepared to endure a blizzard, and I'm not prepared for it either," the announcer said. "As of now I can only see images on the field. I can't describe what I can't see."

Retired Rochester police chief James Macken Jr. told the *Rochester Post-Bulletin* that he remembered watching a punt during the game. The kick went into the strong wind and quickly ended up going backward.

The Rockets beat Winona, 12–6, although few fans stayed to watch the end of the game. The *Post-Bulletin* reported that conditions were bad enough that visitors from Winona could not leave and drive home. They had to find accommodations in Rochester hotels or homes for the night and return to Winona after the storm cleared on Tuesday.

ANOTHER STORY FROM THE day with a football connection involved a fourteen-year-old hunter named Bud who went out with a friend his own age and an older friend who worked as a barber. They were hunting near Yellow Lake near Siren, Wisconsin. The barber stayed at a cabin while the other two went out. They hunted a while but decided to return to the cabin when the snowfall became thick. They struggled, then got disoriented, according to an account in the *Rochester Post-Bulletin*. They heard a train and knew the cabin was near the tracks.

Bud's partner said he could go no farther, so Bud returned to the cabin and started a fire to warm up. The barber went back and helped the other boy back to the cabin. The three stood by the fire until they were warm, then set out in a car to drive home. They got stranded and spent the night in the car.

In the morning, Bud was the only one with dry boots, so he set out and walked three miles to a country store. The telephone was down, so Bud was afraid his friends had died in the storm. They assumed the same about him.

It was two days before they all learned that through different means of help, they had all survived. Bud Grant lived through the blizzard and eventually became the head coach of the Minnesota Vikings in 1967.

Gunnar Miller from Cannon Falls and Walter Prigge from Red Wing were living in Lewiston near Winona on the day of the blizzard. They had gone out about noon that day, hunting in a swampy area not far from Winona. By four o'clock, they realized the weather was changing and decided to leave.

"All at once there came this terrific storm," Miller said in an article in the *Cannon Falls Beacon* in 1979. "The wind was so terrific it took the air right out of your lungs. You couldn't breathe."

The motor on their boat froze, so they paddled to an island. When they reached the island, they met two other hunters, and the four of them worked together to build a wind shelter. Prigge had matches, so they built a fire. Later, around ten o'clock, another hunter saw their fire and joined them. They spent the night keeping the fire going and helping each other stay awake.

"We tried to keep everyone awake," Prigge said. "If you fall asleep you can freeze to death and not even know it."

In the morning, they discovered two other hunters frozen to death just a few hundred yards from the bonfire.

"If we had known they were there, we could have saved them," Prigge said.

On the morning of the thirteenth, rescue parties were moving out. One of the hunters with Prigge and Miller had a father on the Winona police force. He knew where his son was hunting, so he arrived at the island. The river was choppy, so Miller and Prigge decided not to crowd into the boat. The rescue boat left, but waves soon killed its motor.

About that time, Winona airplane pilot Max Conrad flew overhead in his Piper Cub training plane. He saw the stranded boat and flew over it, directing other rescuers to that location. Then he spotted Miller and Prigge and flew over them, opening his plane door and shouting, "Sit tight, boys. Help is on the way," according to Miller.

By noon, another boat had picked up Miller and Prigge, and they returned to their car and drove home.

Conrad, however, was not finished. He was an experienced pilot who, throughout his career, set several distance flying records and completed many transoceanic flights. He was one of the outstanding pilots in the region if not the world.

A story by Chester Whitehorn in the August 1952 issue of *Saga Magazine* described Conrad's departure for his search-and-rescue flights on November 12, 1940.

Max Conrad, in a photo likely taken in the 1950s, flew several flights over stretches of the Mississippi River the day after the blizzard to locate stranded hunters and direct rescue teams to them. *Courtesy of the Winona County Historical Society.*

The article tells how Conrad, in spite of warnings from friends, decided to take off and see if he could help find stranded duck hunters. The wind was still blowing hard, so assistants helped Conrad get his plane out of the hangar. They then pushed against the wings to help the small plane gain speed.

"The crazy little Piper didn't fly—it floated," Whitehorn wrote. "It went straight up, not forward, not like something with a motor, but rising the way a kite does, in dreamy slow motion with Max feeling certain that he was floating backwards, about to crash tail first against the top of the hangar. Then the whirling prop seemed to gain a grip on the wind and Max was in a plane again instead of a kite. He headed out toward the river."

At one point, Conrad saw a dog running around and then noticed small mounds about the size of graves. Then one of the mounds raised an arm and waved.

"Max turned and came back, roaring down again over the mounds. He could make them out definitely now, men lying there covered with ice and snow. He thought it odd for a moment that except for the one who had waved, the men seemed to have no heads," Whitehorn wrote. "And then he felt sick, realizing why. It wasn't solid ground under the mounds, it was shallow water, frozen by the storm. The men's heads were frozen into the ice."

Conrad dropped a bundle of food and then headed back to tell rescue crews where the men were.

SCREAMING WIND

La Crosse schoolteacher Ray Sherin was fourteen years old when he went out hunting the day of the blizzard. He spent the night on an island, freezing. He later wrote: "We had little sense of time and hardly talked. I shivered for what seemed like hours. I prayed silently. I didn't think much about dying. The thing I remember best was the unending scream of the wind. The sound of distant gunshots reached us several times and far-off yells for help," according to a 2010 article in the *La Crosse Tribune*.

Sherin was rescued the next day after Conrad spotted his party. He had an extended stay in the hospital afterward, losing some of his toes to frostbite. He died in 2005.

Harold Eastman of Winona, superintendent of the meter department of the Mississippi Valley Public Service Company, passed away in January 1950. He had served in World War I and received a medal from the National Safety Council for saving the life of a coworker who had been shocked by power lines.

Eastman's obituary in the *Winona Republican-Herald* stated: "Mr. Eastman was one of the hunters marooned up the river from Winona during the Armistice Day Blizzard of November 11, 1940, and was given up for dead at one time. He was rescued the following day chiefly through the efforts of Max Conrad who spotted Eastman and his companion on an island over which Conrad was flying his plane."

In a story written by *Milwaukee Journal* reporter Gordon McQuarrie on November 13 and reprinted in the *Winona Republican-Herald* in 1954, Eastman told his own story.

"I was hunting with R.J. Rice and Richard Guelzer. The wind caught us on a bog. The oarlock broke. Dick said, 'We camp here.' We turned up the skiff for a windbreak. We tried to light a fire, but everything was wet and it was too windy. At 9:30 a.m. Tuesday, we heard a plane. We fired our guns. The plane did not see us. At noon the plane saw us. It was Conrad. I know him. He saved our lives."

Conrad flew over the group and dropped a box of food and supplies. Then he yelled out the door of his plane, "Start out and go in the direction I am."

Eastman and his companions set out, following the direction set by Conrad. They were unsure about walking on the ice.

"We broke through the ice several times," he said, "then we would hang onto the skiff and work it along to new ice. The *Throckmorton* picked us up."

CONRAD DID NOT TAKE all the credit himself. In May 1942, he wrote a letter to the editor of the *Winona Republican Herald.*

> *Cal Volkel was widely known as a superb welder and sheet metal worker, but he should be remembered as the real hero of the Armistice day blizzard. It was Cal who, on that stormy night, took a rowboat alone up the river, encouraged stranded hunters, urged them to keep awake and active, helping them build fires, and brought back as many as he could in the little boat.*
>
> *Half frozen himself after several trips, he went to the airport for winter flying clothes, and continued his rescue work. Early the next morning, with no rest, it was Cal who directed the ground crew who made it possible for us to fly.*
>
> *He was one of the staunchest friends the airport ever had from its earliest days.*

Volkel had left at nine o'clock Tuesday morning to search for Eddie Whitten. Volkel went to town to get Al Squires to go with him. The pair set out with a twelve-horse outboard, and it swamped. They pulled out two sets of oars and, counting to keep time, rowed toward an island, according to McQuarrie's article in the *Winona Republican-Herald.*

"Our backs became ice coated," Volkel said. "I had put on an aviator's suit. We got to the place I knew Eddie was hunting. There were sixteen others there! We got Eddie back ashore and called the police for help. We needed good oarsmen. The men on the island were lying on top of the fire. Not beside it. On top of it."

With most of the firewood wet or buried, the men had been walking around looking for dead branches in trees and then shooting them with their shotguns to break them off. Vogel rowed back to the island with a hatchet and some whiskey. He loaded a man named Anderson in his boat and rowed him to shore. In order to spread the work and danger around, they developed a system.

"Every man who got back ashore in the rowboat went back and took off another, and the one he took off went back and took the next," Volkel told McQuarrie.

WHITEHORN REPORTED THAT CONRAD flew more than a dozen flights over a fifteen-hour period that day, logging some five hundred miles surveying the Mississippi River islands and shores.

Conrad, who with his wife, Betty, had ten children, did not stop with flying rescue missions after the blizzard. He had a long, distinguished career

A view of snowfall along the west side of Main Street between Second and Third Streets in Winona. *Courtesy of the Winona County Historical Society.*

as a pilot, particularly with smaller planes. In 1965, the *Winona Daily News* reported that Conrad had logged over 45,000 hours of flying and had made at least 129 North Atlantic crossings. He had set a long list of records, including a nonstop distance record from Los Angeles to New York, a nonstop distance record of 6,967 miles from Casablanca to El Paso, the first light plane nonstop from New York to Paris and a round-the-world speed record of eight days, 18 hours. In 1954, he completed what he called a Paul Revere flight, visiting all forty-eight state capitals.

He had several close calls, including an emergency landing on the Greenland icecap, but his worst injury happened when his airplane was on the ground. A woman walked into the spinning propeller on his airplane, and Conrad attempted to save her.

"The woman died and Conrad was struck in the head by the prop," reported the *Rochester Post Bulletin* in 1979. "The injuries blanked out his memory for three years, and he had to learn to talk again."

During his career, Conrad trained numerous other pilots and started a youth project called the Winona Experiment to foster teenage interest in aviation. In 1965, he received the Harmon Trophy, one of the highest honors in aviation, and in 1961, the Winona Airport was renamed Max Conrad Field.

6
THE WINDS OF HELL

O n the morning of November 12, the Goodhue County Sheriff's Office noted that forty to fifty people were still missing. That day's edition of the *Red Wing Daily Republican* devoted the entire front page and several interior pages to developments of the storm and the plight of those trapped outside in it. Photos of rescued duck hunters enjoying a warm meal at a local restaurant ran alongside stories of abandoned cars, missing people, missing boats, car wrecks, reports of snow depths and low temperatures, as well as damage done by wind and snow.

Only hours after it began, the storm was being called one of the worst blizzards in Minnesota history. It shut down highways, blocked supply trucks and bus service and left many travelers waiting for hours or days before they could reach their destinations. Rural electric lines in several places, including Zumbrota, were reported out of commission. Mail carriers were heading out on routes, knowing they would not be able to make all deliveries.

One article reported that Highways 61 and 58 were closed by deep snowdrifts, and no one could predict how long it might take to restore movement on them.

"The newspaper, bread and other trucks, which usually arrive here early each morning, failed to make an appearance, it being reported that the state highway department had made no efforts to open up the roads because of the stiff wind, which formed drifts almost as quickly as they could be removed."

J.A. Prior, the Goodhue County highway engineer, noted that rural highways were "unquestionably sealed by drifts in various sections of the county, but that no reports had been received from snowplow operators, who

The day after the blizzard, the *Red Wing Daily Republican* carried multiple stories about the tragedy that had developed the previous afternoon and night. *Courtesy of the Goodhue County Historical Society.*

were attempting to open them up so that some semblance of transportation could be restored."

The Milwaukee Road railroad was able to keep its trains running through the night. The Chicago Great Western Railway was able to move its regular freight train but held the passenger train in Red Wing waiting further reports of track conditions. The main train from the Twin Cities to Kansas City had been stopped at Kenyon while crews tried to remove deep drifts from the tracks.

Within Red Wing, "The city crew swung into service in opening up the city streets after the storm had abated enough to make it possible to operate the plows without danger of running into cars obscured by the blinding snow. A sizeable crew of men was engaged in clearing of the streets, and it was expected much of the work would be completed by tomorrow noon."

THE *RED WING DAILY Republican*, the *Winona Republican Herald*, the *Rochester Post Bulletin* and other area papers carried stories about those missing and those confirmed dead. The plight of local duck hunters grabbed the most attention, but many other people were affected by the storm or its tragic results.

One hundred people were involved in a massive wreck of more than thirty cars near New Brighton on the northern side of the Twin Cities. A dozen or more people were injured by flying glass.

"The jam started when an automobile collided with a White Bear–Stillwater bus," the *Star Tribune* reported from its history archives. "Three more cars piled into the bus, and one of them sideswiped an oncoming car in the opposite traffic lane. Within a short time two dozen other motorists, blinded by the snow, slid into the pile of disabled machines."

The *Daily Republican* reported a car wreck four miles from Zumbrota that sent four people to the hospital, and the *Post Bulletin* noted a family of four who left Mankato and "became lost in the blizzard a mile outside of town. The car was buried in snow and when it was found two days later, three of the four family members had frozen to death."

The sudden change in weather on November 11, 1940, left motorists, hunters and many others stranded in what came to be known as the Armistice Day Blizzard. *Courtesy of the Goodhue County Historical Society.*

On Tuesday, the *Republican Herald* noted that five people had been taken to the local hospital with frozen hands and feet. The article listed several people known dead, including Fred Nyles, Herman Pagel, Carl W. Tarras, Herbert Juenemann, Theodore Henry Geiger and Clyde J. Deira.

"It will be several days before a full check of the death toll of the storm can be definitely established," the article read. "There are still several unclaimed automobiles parked in different parts of the area."

The *Republican Herald* ran an article on Wednesday reporting that "Some of the victims froze to death in stalled automobiles, thousands of which dotted the highways, others became lost or exhausted while battling the blinding snow, and some died in traffic accidents."

The dead included Mrs. E.Y. Arnold of St. Paul, who was killed in a car-truck collision near Stillwater. Walter Strom from Minneapolis, a Soo Line railway fireman, was killed in a collision between a freight train and a passenger train at Watkins. John C. Johnson (fifty-five) of Minneapolis and Harry S. Mason (seventy-nine) of St. Paul both died of exhaustion. Richard Lee Marden (fifty) of Minneapolis collapsed and died after shoveling snow. Mrs. Thurzla Cotew (eighty-one) of Fairmont was found dead in the entry of her home. Similar lists appeared in area papers, and the lists continued to grow as search-and-rescue crews persisted.

The U.S. War Department boat *Throckmorton* had gone out several times from Fountain City to look for stranded hunters in the river as well as to recover bodies and pick up equipment, dogs and anything else it could find that hunters might have left behind.

THE FORCES OF THE Armistice Day Blizzard affected not only humans but also livestock and wildlife. Animals were buried in snowdrifts and frozen in the wet, cold conditions. Thousands of animals died, but a few stories had somewhat better endings.

The *Winona Republican Herald* reported on November 19 that Otto Berberich, a farmer near Courtland, west of Mankato, thought he had lost 1,500 turkeys. After the storm settled, he went out to a snowbank where he believed many turkeys had been buried and found that most of them were still alive beneath the snow. He dug them out. In the end, he estimated that he lost 600 turkeys instead of the entire flock.

"Outside of being hungry, the turkeys apparently came through the snow imprisonment with no ill effects," the *Republican Herald* reported.

Thousands of turkeys died in the blizzard on farms in the Rochester area. Many were smothered; others were frozen.

"Health officials later ruled that sale of frozen turkeys for human consumption was illegal," the *Post Bulletin* reported.

Near Red Wing, Sam Strandemo was out on his farm three days after the storm and noticed steam coming from a straw stack, according to Frank Callister, writing in the *Red Wing Republican Eagle* in 1977.

"He shoveled a path to the stack and dug around in the straw," Callister explained. "Suddenly about fifty squealing pigs emerged from this snow-covered prison none the worse for their long period of fasting."

Minnesota beekeepers survived the blizzard with small losses, according to Charles S. Hofman of Janesville, president of the Minnesota Beekeepers Association. The bees, he said, know how to huddle.

"When the temperature inside the hive drops to 57 degrees," Hofman told the *Winona Republican-Herald*, "the bees form a cluster about a honey comb. As it gets colder, they contract this cluster tighter and tighter. Thermometers forced into the center of such a cluster have shown a temperature of 93 degrees."

GALLOPING WINDS

The storm that became the Armistice Day Blizzard in Southeast Minnesota began several days earlier in the Pacific Northwest. It roared into Washington State on November 7 and destroyed the Tacoma Narrows Bridge, the third-longest suspension span in the world.

"The Tacoma Narrows Bridge, an engineering wonder, had already acquired the name Galloping Gertie due to its motion in the wind," according to the National Weather Service. "A four mile-an-hour breeze could start oscillations in the bridge while stronger breezes often had no effect. On November 7, 1940, winds of thirty-five to forty-five mph caused the center span to undulate three to five feet and the bridge failed before the center of the storm system reached shore."

The storm moved southeast and crossed the Rocky Mountains, re-forming over Trinidad, Colorado. It then moved east to Iowa before curving north. It created blizzards in South Dakota and an ice storm in Nebraska before it turned to head up the Mississippi River valley. The National Weather Service reported that gale-force winds of eighty miles per hour hit Grand Rapids, Michigan, and the winds may have been even harder over the lakes.

Meteorologist Paul Douglas with WCCO in Minneapolis, speaking with MPRNews, said, "It hit the Pacific Northwest with near hurricane-force gusts. Usually storms weaken somewhat as they cross the Rockies, but this storm did not weaken. In fact, as it tapped moisture from the Gulf of Mexico and cold air lurking just north over Canada, the two combined into an explosive pattern, and the storm system really became what meteorologists call a bomb."

Douglas said the storm passed near Des Moines, Iowa, and then north toward Eau Claire, Wisconsin. He explained that the low barometric pressure caused the moist air from the south and the cold air from the north to interact, and "those two converged to produce this incredible intensification to the point where you really did have what you could call an inland hurricane."

The National Weather Service (NWS) stated that by the time the storm reached Lake Superior, the barometric reading had dropped to 28.57 inches of mercury. The extreme low pressure created the severe weather conditions of that day and helped bring in the storm that had first attacked the Tacoma Narrows Bridge then swept across a thousand miles of the heartland.

"Across the upper Midwest drifts up to twenty feet high buried cars and rescuers had to force long probes into the rock hard drifts in their search for missing people," reported the NWS. "Passenger trains were stranded and roads and highways remained closed for days. Newspaper deliveries were halted; telephone and power lines were damaged as were homes, barns, and outbuildings in Minnesota, Wisconsin, Illinois, Iowa, and Michigan."

The high winds caused many shipwrecks, yet the crews went out, because there was high demand for the products they carried, such as coal and food.

"Mariners, aware of the dangers on the Great Lakes, paid close attention to the weather," said the National Weather Service. "But during the Armistice Day storm many of the crews were unaware that the winds would shift until their ships were struck broadside by the full force of the wind. During the storm three large ships sank near Pentwater, Michigan, and fifty-eight lives were lost. Survivors on ships that ran aground waited for days on their damaged vessels until winds subsided and rescue boats could be launched from shore. Communities expecting the cargos for their winter supplies were significantly impacted by the loss of food and fuel."

With so many people surprised by the power and suddenness of the blizzard, concerns about the weather-reporting system became common. In 1940, weather was reported by regional offices. The office in Chicago covered most of the Upper Midwest.

"Perhaps the most embarrassing revelation was that no one was watching the storm's explosive development in the pre-dawn hours of November 11," said the MPRNews report. "A retired government forecaster says the Midwest headquarters in Chicago was not staffed overnight. The uproar led to several changes. The Chicago office went to round-the-clock operation, and the Twin Cities branch was upgraded so it could issue forecasts."

Within days of the Armistice Day Blizzard, Minnesota governor Harold E. Stassen contacted Secretary of Commerce Jesse Jones in Washington, complaining that poor weather warnings had contributed to the devastation of the previous weekend, according to the *Winona Republican Herald* of March 19, 1940.

The *Republican Herald* called for an expansion of weather bureau facilities in the Twin Cities and elsewhere throughout the region to help decrease the effects of future storms. "The Northwest may go for many years without another of these storms," wrote the paper, "but it needs every possible means of giving warnings which might be helpful."

A view of snowfall in Winona along West Third Street between Johnson and Main along the south side of the street. *Courtesy of the Winona County Historical Society.*

As a result, many more weather offices have been opened across the country, giving citizens a much more local version of the forecast.

Douglas of WCCO said that technology has helped the accuracy of today's forecasts. Even with those improvements, "there can still be scenarios where we are surprised, where we are caught and that's why this can be such a humbling profession," he said.

In addition to better technology for forecasting, the NWS relies on huge collections of data to help determine weather patterns. It also counts on thousands of weather spotters, people trained by NWS meteorologists to recognize the signs of severe weather.

"Storm spotters are important, because their reports provide the real time account of what is actually happening," said Donna Dubberke, meteorologist at the NWS forecast office in La Crosse, Wisconsin, in the *Red Wing Republican Eagle* in 2020. "It is part of what we call the integrated warning process."

Storm spotters are asked to report such information as the amount of rainfall, the size of hail, the types of clouds forming, wind gusts and any damage they may know about. By having spotters throughout the coverage region, the NWS can use the data from reports to determine how a storm is developing, where it is moving and what type of threat it might bring. From that, it can issue warnings, if needed, and add information to its weather records.

The reports from storm spotters are important to the NWS, because those reports "go into the warning decisions," Dubberke said. "We share them with the media and others so that people in the path of the storm know what to expect."

All of that would have been incredibly important information for the hundreds of duck hunters and stranded travelers who were out in the elements on November 11, 1940.

"The Armistice Day Storm remains noteworthy to society because it was a seminal event that continues to impact humans," wrote the NWS. "Anything that endures as part of a culture from one generation to another is considered a seminal event; and the societal impacts of such an event can change lives and change history. The consequences of societal impacts alter the ways in which people live, work, play, relate to one another, organize to meet their needs, and generally cope as members of society. Forecasters must assess the potential for societal impacts when they strive to understand the atmospheric environment, timing of an event, and the social environment in their warning areas."

The impacts of the blizzard linger today.

"Evidence of the Armistice Day Blizzard is recorded in newspaper clippings, photos, museum collections, and stories of this event have been captured in cookbooks, journal articles, and passed on through family oral traditions," wrote the NWS. "This storm produced an impact on society due to the death and destruction left in its wake. If one measures the impact of an event by the diversity of the information that remains, this storm was indeed memorable."

The *Rochester Post Bulletin* reported that, in the end, the blizzard killed 154 people throughout the Upper Midwest, including 49 in Minnesota. The snow depths reached as much as 16.0 inches in the Twin Cities; the highest depth was 26.6 inches, reported in Collegeville, west of the Twin Cities.

THE INVISIBLE FORCE

In the dramatic prose of the day, Gordon McQuarrie, in his *Milwaukee Journal* article, captured the emotion of November 11 and its immediate aftermath.

> *The winds of Hell were loose on the Mississippi Armistice Day and night.*
> *They came across the prairie, from the south and west, a mighty freezing, invisible force. They charged down from the river bluffs to the placid stream below and reached with deathly fingers for the life that beat beneath the canvas jackets of thousands of duck hunters.*
> *They will tell of this for years to come. They will recall how Dad and Mother were saved, and men who came through it alive together will look at each other with new understanding, as is the way with those who have seen death brush them close.*

He went on to personify the storm and its actions.

> *The wind did it. The cold was its ally. Mother Nature, sometimes a blue-eyed girl with corn-colored hair, was a murderous mistress Tuesday night on the Mississippi.*
> *She caught thousands of duck hunters on Armistice Day—a holiday. She teased them out to the river and the marshes with her fine, whooping wind and then when she got them there, she froze them like muskrats in traps. She promised ducks in the wind. They came, all right. The survivors tell that grimly, but by that time the duck hunters of the Mississippi were playing a bigger game—with their lives at stake.*

Owen Redman, who with his friend Arnold Vogel went to Colvill Park in Red Wing at noon and decided not to go hunting that day, was lucky. He and Vogel did get involved in rescue missions that night but weren't trapped on islands in the Mississippi River like so many other hunters. Talking to the *Republican Eagle* in 1990 about that day, Redman said he had been in other storms, but "I don't recall one that broke that fast."

PART III

THE FLOOD OF 1965

7

THE SILENT SIEGE

Compared to a raging tornado or a blinding blizzard that delivers destruction in hours or perhaps minutes, the Mississippi River Flood of 1965 moved in slow motion. It crept in, rising steadily day after day, forcing officials to revise again and again their predictions of when it would peak and when it would recede.

Along the Mississippi and dozens of tributaries, fear and anxiety rose with the water levels. People worried about their homes, their businesses, their communities and their futures.

The *Red Wing Daily Republican Eagle* referred to the flood as "The Silent Siege." That siege was the product of several factors that created the perfect flood, according to the National Weather Service. Starting in late November 1964 and lasting through Christmas, temperatures averaged three to seven degrees below normal, and through most of that time, there was no snowfall throughout the region.

With no snow as insulation, those early cold temperatures drove frost deep into the ground. When the snow did arrive, it rested on the frozen ground until a warming came late in February.

According to the U.S. Department of the Interior in a report titled *Floods of March–May 1965 in the Upper Mississippi River Basin* by D.B. Anderson and I.L. Burmeister:

> *Throughout most of the upper Mississippi River basin, flooding occurred during two separate periods almost a month apart. During the first period*

A sign asking people to "Wipe your feet" seems a bit misplaced during the historic flood. *Courtesy of the Goodhue County Historical Society.*

warm temperatures during the latter part of February and early March melted the winter's accumulation of snow in southeastern Minnesota, northeastern Iowa, southwestern Wisconsin. The runoff from snowmelt and rainfall, which in some areas exceeded two inches during the first three days of March, caused severe flooding in the Zumbro and Root River basins in Minnesota and in the Cedar River basin in Minnesota and Iowa.

Then a series of winter storms dumped heavy snow throughout the region, and temperatures dropped significantly. "March of 1965 was one of the coldest Marches ever recorded in both Minnesota and Wisconsin," wrote the NWS. "These colder temperatures prevented the gradual melting and runoff of the snowpack."

When the snow finally did begin to melt, it kept the Mississippi River at high levels. That was further enhanced by high waters coming into the Mississippi from the Minnesota, St. Croix, Rush, Cannon, Zumbro, Root and Chippewa Rivers, as well as many other tributaries.

The final blow came when as much as 3.5 inches of rain fell on the region during the first two weeks of April, most of it from April 3 to 7. "Normally the rain would sink into the ground," the NWS explained. "However, with the frozen ground the rain had no place to go other than into streams and rivers. In addition, the rain melted the abnormally deep snow pack, resulting in even more water."

The Department of the Interior report explained that the second period of flooding started in early April and extended into May throughout the entire upper Mississippi River basin.

"These floods were caused by the rapid melting of the winter's accumulation of snow in northern Minnesota and Wisconsin and the March accumulation of snow in northern Iowa, southern Minnesota and Wisconsin," the report stated.

The water equivalent of snow in the upper part of the basin was as much as eleven inches. Warm temperatures moved northward into Minnesota during the last days of March and nighttime temperatures remained above freezing. As much as three inches of rain fell during the period April 3–7;

Looking north at Bear Creek near C25 and Fourth Street Southeast in Rochester. *Courtesy of the History Center of Olmsted County.*

*it accelerated the snowmelt and increased the runoff. Frost penetrated the
ground deeply, as a result of the severe winter, and consequently much of the
rain and snowmelt ran off. Those streams which flooded early in March,
flooded again, but this time more extensively. Many of the streams which
were covered by snow and ice in March were raging torrents in full flood
in April.*

RAIN, SLEET AND SNOW

For many communities in the region, the two parts were not much separated.
March opened with a storm dumping rain, sleet and snow in southeast
Minnesota, especially on Rochester, Zumbro Falls, Kenyon, Wanamingo,
Hammond, Millville, Welch and Cannon Falls. Several roads were damaged,
schools were closed and homes were flooded. Telephone poles and trees
were cut down by ice chunks.

Residents of Rochester had been receiving warnings of an impending
storm. They were advised to listen to their radios for updates from the U.S.
Weather Bureau, which promised frequent advisories. Law enforcement,
civil defense authorities and Red Cross officials were all watching
the situation.

Mayor Alex Smekta told the *Rochester Post Bulletin* that "all city resources,"
including off-duty police, fire and public utility department personnel, were
ready if the flood developed as forecasted.

Police Chief James J. Macken Jr. urged residents to stay away from deep-
water areas and to monitor their children.

On Monday, March 1, both the Zumbro River and Bear Creek roared out
of their banks and inundated several sections of Rochester. At least thirty
people were forced to evacuate their homes, but no injuries were reported.
Damage to homes and businesses was estimated in the thousands of dollars.

Many people in southeast Rochester were unable to go home or were
forced to wade through waist-deep water to reach their houses. Car owners
were moving their vehicles from behind the Mayo Civic Auditorium as the
river moved into the parking lot. In some locations in Rochester, ice chunks
were jamming culverts and blocking runoff.

The *Winona Daily News* reported that one of the problems for Rochester
was that "many of the homes flooded on the lowlands there have been
constructed in the boom years of that community. The river was narrowed
by crowding it into a smaller area."

Photograph of the residential area in northwest Rochester, taken from Ninth Avenue Northwest, showing the west side of Ninth Avenue Northwest just north of Fifth Street Northwest. *Courtesy of the History Center of Olmsted County.*

The problem was made worse by the early cold temperatures that left much of the ground in the area frozen. The *Daily News* explained that "the area around Rochester, as well as all of Southeastern Minnesota, [was] coated with a thin crust of ice that stopped the surface water from seeping into the ground—thus it had to run off into the rivers and creeks, causing one of the more destructive tributary floods in recent years. The ice-crusted ground was like a tin roof."

Communities surrounding Rochester were sharing the same concerns and problems. In Oronoco, the gates on the dam froze and the level of the lake was rising. While officials were working to loosen the gates, word came that an ice jam had blocked Packard's Bridge three miles northwest of town. Increased water building up in both locations caused concern for residents.

West of Rochester, electrical power was out in Manterville, and roads were underwater throughout Dodge County.

At the Rochester Hydro-Electric plant at Lake Zumbro near Mazeppa, crews reported that the Zumbro River had risen by more than three feet, and officials were expecting further increases.

Floodwater crashes against the Oronoco bridge. *Courtesy of the History Center of Olmsted County.*

Near Zumbrota, two school buses slid off the road, one because of ice and the other because of mud. No injuries were reported.

South of Rochester, schools in Lanesboro were closed, and the Root River was rising. It increased by a foot at 11:00 a.m. in Preston and covered the Whalen Bridge. It spilled out of its banks in several places near Chatfield, covering flatlands.

Radio station WCCO in Minneapolis reported that it had covered more than 250 school closings either because of or in anticipation of the storms and flooding.

Robert Babb, meteorologist with the U.S. Weather Bureau, said that Rochester was lucky that at least 20 percent of the snow and ice in the area did not melt. He said that if temperatures had been five degrees higher over the weekend, more snow and ice would have melted, and the resulting flooding would have been much greater.

Waters throughout the area continued to rise until the afternoon, when temperatures dropped and slowed the increase.

Babb told the Rochester *Post Bulletin* that cold air had arrived in "the nick of time" on Monday, causing much of the rain that fell in the afternoon to freeze, lowering the flood level by as much as half a foot.

"The whole purpose in issuing a flood warning is to prevent the loss of life and property," Babb said. "In this case, we were lucky to be able to warn persons well in advance, so they could take precautions to keep property damage to a minimum."

The *Post Bulletin* reported that "the Zumbro River crested at 21.2 feet at the Sewage Treatment Plant about 6:30 p.m., a record high stage and 9.2 feet over bankful. At the South Beltline, the Zumbro reached a crest of 9.3 at 6:30 p.m., three-tenths of a foot over flood stage, but luckily some two feet less than had first been forecast."

In the Department of the Interior report, Anderson and Burmeister stated: "Most streams in Minnesota crested in April, but a few streams in the southeastern part of the state, crested in early March. The Zumbro River, which flows into the Mississippi River downstream from Lake Pepin and Lock and Dam 4, is the northernmost of these streams."

The Zumbro River peaked on March 1, during the first round of precipitation. The Department of the Interior added, "Another peak occurred on April 7, but the April flooding was not as severe because the winter snow cover had already melted and run off during the March flood."

The March 1 crest had come quickly, and locals were happy to hear the news.

"Homeowners and businessmen affected by flood waters spent anxious moments Monday afternoon and evening and breathed sighs of relief with the rest of the community when word came about nine p.m. that the Zumbro and Bear were starting to recede," the *Post Bulletin* reported.

Firemen in Rochester use a boat to try to reach stranded citizens. *Courtesy of the History Center of Olmsted County.*

As residents began the process of cleaning up, the Rochester–Olmsted County Health Department released guidelines to help with water and food quality. It assured Rochester residents that the city water supply was safe but cautioned those with private wells to monitor the color of the water and to follow a process of cleaning the wells with bleach. It also recommended destroying any food that had been contaminated by floodwaters, as well as cleaning walls and floors thoroughly if they were affected by the deluge.

FARTHER SOUTH, THE ROOT River near Lanesboro and Rushford, south of Winona, caused extensive damage in Rushford and Houston. The Red Cross in Rochester reported that half the town of Rushford, population six hundred, was underwater. The Red Cross estimated that 75 to 90 percent of the 373 homes in Houston had been seriously damaged, reported the *Post Bulletin*.

"Runoff from snowmelt started in the Root River basin at the end of February," according to the U.S. Department of the Interior, "as the result of warm temperatures and was intensified by a heavy rain which fell on March 1. This condition created very sharp ice-affected peaks in the basin on March 1 and 2. Stages exceeded any previously known from Lanesboro, Minn., to the mouth."

THE WATER WAS RECEDING in Rochester and the surrounding area, but the threat wasn't over. With the dropping temperatures, the rain turned to sleet, then snow. Areas of southern Minnesota reported several inches of snow and winds up to fifty miles per hour blowing the snow into deep drifts.

The low temperatures, snow and rising water soon affected the small town of Welch, on the Cannon River. On March 4, the *Daily Republican Eagle* reported that a large ice jam had formed in the bend of the river about one half mile downstream from the Welch bridge, causing concerns that it might release and cause damage to farmland and property.

County engineer Roy Carls said the river would have to get much deeper to float the ice dam out, and the location of the dam made it very difficult to consider blasting. "There isn't much we can do about it," he told the *Daily Republican Eagle*, explaining that the main threat was that if the ice dam broke, the water could wash away topsoil and create erosion gullies on farmland.

HEAVY SNOWFALL

At that time, Carls's attitude might have been justified, because that first storm passed by and subsided. Then snow covered the area.

"Heavy snowfall continued throughout March," noted the Department of the Interior. "A blizzard on March 17–18 spread over northern Iowa, Wisconsin, Minnesota, and eastern South Dakota depositing up to eighteen inches of snow. The snow on the ground after this storm totaled up to forty-five inches in the upper Rum, Snake, and Kettle River basins in Minnesota."

The National Weather Service defined the snows as a series of storms occurring on March 1–3, March 10–12, March 17–18 and March 27–29. The heaviest snows fell in the Minnesota River valley with ranges of 14.1 inches at Tyler to 58.0 inches at Bird Island. Most locations saw snow averages of from 30.0 to 40.0 inches.

March 1965 was one of the coldest months on record, noted the National Weather Service. From 1901 to 2000, Minnesota had an average March temperature of 26.0 degrees, but in 1965, the average was 14.8 degrees, some 11.2 degrees colder than normal. It was the second-coldest March in recorded history, after March 1899, which had an average temperature of 13.3 degrees.

The frigid temperatures throughout March drove frost deep into the ground. The Department of the Interior said that in the upper basin, where deep snow existed, frost penetration was about one foot, but farther south, where little snow existed, frost penetrated as much as five feet.

"There was heavy precipitation during the first part of March, followed by below freezing temperatures which reached the subzero range during the period March 19–26," the department reported. "In some areas, there was a layer of ice on the ground from the storm on March 1 and previous storms. The frozen ground covered with glaze was a very important factor in intensifying the spring flood of 1965."

The U.S. Weather Bureau issued its first official flood warning on March 19, noting that the river at Red Wing and Lake City could reach fourteen feet, the level of flood stage. It said that if the melt and runoff took three or more days, flooding would not be bad, but if it happened faster, that would increase the problems and the depth of the flooding.

Many people in the area could easily remember 1952, when the river reached a record of 16.8 feet. The mid-March warnings of 1965 didn't scare them too much, but by the beginning of April, feelings were changing.

With the floodwaters too high, towboats were tied up at the levee in Red Wing. *Courtesy of the Goodhue County Historical Society.*

On April 7, the Cannon River was overflowing its banks. Munson Implement Inc. in Cannon Falls reported that most of its implements were underwater. The Cannon River crested at 12.56 feet the morning of April 6, dropped several inches, then crested a second time on the morning of April 7.

The runoff just above Welch on the Cannon River was the highest recorded at any of the more than one hundred gauging stations in Minnesota, according to the U.S. Department of the Interior. It added: "The maximum discharge of 36,100 cubic feet per second at the Welch gauging station on April 8 was more than twice that of the 1952 flood and 1.54 times the discharge of a fifty-year flood."

The Zumbro River was ten feet over flood stage at Zumbro Falls on April 6 and crested at twelve feet over flood stage on April 7.

The Vermillion River in Hastings burst out of its banks on April 6 and sent 281 families from their homes. One square mile, forty-two city blocks, of the southwestern section of Westwood in Hastings was inundated.

"Flooding started about four a.m. Tuesday when the normally peaceful Vermillion sought a new channel for itself right through Westwood," reported the *Daily Republican Eagle*. "Basements were flooded. Basement walls came crashing down, cars were submerged and fences were carried off.

Only the houses themselves were visible as streets and lawns were obscured by the rushing flood waters."

Electricity and natural gas were shut off to the area, and hundreds of policemen, firemen, civil defense workers and volunteers—some working more than twenty-four consecutive hours—joined in the effort to assist in the evacuation.

The crest of the Vermillion River on April 6 caused at least $750,000 in damage, according to the Department of the Interior. In contrast, the crest of the Mississippi River in Hastings two weeks later, on April 18, caused $50,000 in damage.

Two deaths were caused by flooding in Minnesota on April 6. An eight-year-old boy, Loren Meyer, drowned in a creek on the family farm near Marshall. Freeman Sammons, thirty-nine, of Tracy was working on a bridge near Jackson when he fell into the river filled with chunks of ice and disappeared.

IN THE TWIN CITIES, the surging Mississippi River was quick to cause problems. The metropolitan sewage treatment plant had saved a lot of money by not using expensive pumping stations, relying instead on gravity to move the sewage into the plant, according to a 2019 report published by the Metropolitan Waste Control Commission. On April 8, the river level reached a point where it was above the outfall. The plant was forced to shut down.

Workers placed sandbags around the facility and struggled to repair leaks. By April 11, a crew of forty-one was working on the site when the floating debris and ice made it impossible for the workers to leave Pig Island and return to the shore. They were stranded there for the next twelve days.

That was not the only problem. With the sewage plant shut down, many expressed concerns about water quality and safety. The *Daily Republican Eagle* reported that area wells should be "considered unsafe until flood waters recede and wells are tested for bacteria content. The chance of water borne disease appears considerable since the shutdown Thursday of the Twin Cities Metropolitan Sewage Treatment Plant in St. Paul. The plant serves the entire metropolitan area including about thirty suburbs. Sewage that normally would be treated at the plant is going into the Mississippi raw."

Flooding near the boathouses at Bay Point in Red Wing. *Courtesy of the Goodhue County Historical Society.*

THE ORIGINAL PREDICTION IN March of 14.0 feet was updated on April 8, and the U.S. Weather Bureau stated that the Mississippi River, which had risen 1.9 feet from the day before, could easily exceed the levels of the 1952 flood.

Now the river had everyone's attention, including that of President Lyndon Johnson, who, at the request of Governor Karl Rolvaag, declared Minnesota a major disaster area on Sunday, April 11. Johnson named thirty-nine counties that needed assistance.

8

WE ALMOST LOST EVERYTHING

ndrella Hansen, who with her husband, Martin, owned Hansen's Harbor, a marina four miles north of Lake City, kept a diary of the flood that she shared with the *Daily Republican Eagle*. She noted that they had become frightened of the rising water and brought in Leo Joyce, a contractor from Rochester, to build a dike at the marina. The Hansens' son Sookie, a civil engineer, had designed the dike, and work crews arrived on April 9 to start work.

Over the next two days, they moved boats to safety. Two dozers and three trucks hauled and placed materials for the dike. On April 12 and 13, everyone available, including friends Dr. and Mrs. John Hodgson from Frontenac, pitched in and made sandbags.

"Making sandbags at ten cents each—cutting in half and making two from each 100 pound feed bag," Andrella wrote. "The Hodgsons were here all day. Mrs. Hodgson and daughters Lori and Amy worked like troupers."

On April 14, she added, "More sandbags. Lake City is out of bags. Hope these are enough—have 500 now."

Also on that day, the Hansens' son Pete, a student at Dunwoody Institute in Minneapolis, came home to help the family fight the flood.

ON THE SAME DAY that the Hansens began work on their dike, Lock and Dam No. 3 just upriver from Red Wing sent out an emergency request for 172,000 sandbags and 3,750 tons of sand. Even though the river was

Above: Carts filled with sandbags arrive on the railroad tracks, and workers get ready to place them. *Courtesy of the Goodhue County Historical Society.*

Opposite: No trains could use the tracks that were well underwater during the Mississippi River flood of 1965. *Courtesy of the Goodhue County Historical Society.*

at 9.63 feet, some 4.5 feet below flood stage, the U.S. Army Corps of Engineers asked for all the labor help it could get, as the U.S. Weather Bureau again adjusted its prediction to a high of 18.0 feet, more than 1.0 foot over the 1952 flood level.

According to the *Daily Republican Eagle*, thirty families were evacuated from Island Road north of Red Wing. Sixty people were removed from Prairie Island, and a dozen families were taken from both Bay City and Wacouta.

Edward Cedarblade, a new resident of Prairie Island, said: "They say you can't really consider yourself an Island resident until you've been flooded out. I guess we're full-fledged residents."

The railroad between St. Paul and La Crosse was closed to both passenger and freight trains.

The sewage plant in Red Wing closed on April 12, reporting that it had fifteen feet of water in the basement.

All along the riverfront, businesses boarded up windows and piled sandbags against the ever-encroaching water. An emergency operations

center for civil defense and Red Cross workers was set up in the courthouse basement in Red Wing to monitor developments with the river.

The U.S. Weather Bureau again increased its prediction, stating that the water level could exceed twenty feet.

ANDRELLA HANSEN EXPRESSED THE anxiety of all those along the Mississippi River in her diary.

> *April 15. Water is 18.7 feet—going to 20.5. Wonder if our dike will hold? More plastic—more sandbags—more gravel. Joyce's crew here from 8 pm to 10 pm then had to go to Winona. Water up six inches in 12 hours. Everyone wore out.*
>
> *April 16—Watching pumps. Have to get gas every few hours. Sandbags, shoveling, moving furniture and shop things. The lumber company picked up my stove, refrigerator and cabinets and mahogany lumber. The neighbor's help is tremendous.*

And the water continued to rise.

THE U.S. WEATHER BUREAU was keeping watch on rising waters caused by abnormal melting along the St. Croix River. That caused hydrologist Joseph Strub to revise the forecast once again and raise the predicted level to 20.5 feet.

Water surrounded the Red Wing railroad depot, and many of the boathouses in the harbor were lifted to the tops of their gin poles.

Crews had been working hard to protect Highway 63 and the bridge from Red Wing to Wisconsin. Finally, on April 16, they had to give up and close the road and bridge, leaving many workers with no way to get to their jobs in Red Wing.

To avoid the long drive to either Hastings or Wabasha to cross a bridge, Red Wing locals made good use of a fishing boat as a ferry. "There was a guy with a big flat-bottom boat, and he brought people back and forth," Howard Rapp told the *Daily Republican Eagle*. "He would bring ten or fifteen people at a time. They could drive over so far and then park on the side of the road and take the boat across."

Water reaches high up the supporting pillars of the Red Wing bridge and the trees nearby. *Courtesy of the Goodhue County Historical Society.*

If passenger demand grew greater, ferry pilots would tow a second boat, allowing them to haul up to forty passengers at one time. The *Daily Republican Eagle* reported that one morning during the ten-day period the highway was closed, more than two hundred cars were parked along the road at the north end of the Back Channel bridge. The ferry dropped passengers off about one hundred yards north of the high bridge in Red Wing, and a city bus was making trips back and forth to shuttle passengers into town and to their jobs.

Handling the ferry across the river fell to the hands of Ernest "Tut" Johnson and Milton Sorenson, with some help from S.C. "Sven" Sorenson, all three from Bay City.

While the ferry was important, in some cases it simply wasn't fast enough. During the road closure, nine patients needed transportation from Wisconsin to the Red Wing hospital. Pilots Jack Selkirk, Bob Cushing and John Stuber of the Red Wing Soaring Association donated their time and skills, sometimes in the middle of the night, to fly patients from the Red Wing airport near Bay City across the river to the Selkirk farm in Wacouta, where they were then driven to the hospital.

SHEET OF ICE

Lake Pepin is the largest lake on the Mississippi River. It is three miles wide and twenty-two miles long, and in the heart of winter, it is covered with ice two feet thick. As the river rose higher and higher in 1965, residents of Lake City feared that a shift in wind could cause a sheet of ice to slice through the marina or the houses and trailers on Central Point and near Ohuta Beach.

"The ice failed to blow against the Lake City point, but Central Point property owners were not as fortunate," reported the *Daily Republican Eagle*. "A strong southeasterly wind pushed the massive ice flow into homes and summer cottages on the point. Walls were tumbled, roofs came down, when buildings were pushed as much as forty feet off their foundations. Total destruction was estimated at nearly fifty percent. Almost all the remaining structures were damaged severely."

Citizens also were concerned about the city's water and sewer systems, so they built large sandbag barricades around those stations.

A DOZEN MILES TO the south, residents of Wabasha had similar concerns about the thick ice on Lake Pepin. An emergency dike was built at the harbor to ward off ice floating down the river. A towboat, the *Ann King*, which had earlier tried to break through the ice on Lake Pepin, positioned itself where it could help break up any approaching ice floes.

Dan Foley, a former national commander of the American Legion, was appointed emergency civil defense director. He devised an evacuation plan for Wabasha residents as well as a communications system. The *Daily Republican Eagle* reported that at the height of the flood, nearly one-third of the residents were affected.

Foley reported that chunks of ice floating downstream were hitting the Wabasha-Nelson bridge, but the "structure is holding firm."

ON APRIL 16, THE U.S. Weather Bureau reported that a drop in temperatures meant that snow and ice melt would be slower than expected, meaning that the expected crest of the Mississippi River would be delayed a day or two, and that workers maintaining dikes and other protective structures would need to hold them in place longer. The bureau expected the river to crest at twenty-five feet in Hastings on April 17, twenty-one feet in Red Wing on April 18 or 19 and twenty-one feet in Winona on April 20. The forecast also noted that the slow river rise indicated that a flat crest hanging on for several hours or even a couple of days was likely.

"There's so much water all over everywhere that it will have to be a slow drop," said Joseph Strub, hydrologist for the U.S. Weather Bureau.

WHILE COMMUNITIES ALONG THE Mississippi River were fighting the battle against the silent siege, communities on tributaries, where river crests had occurred days or weeks earlier, started looking ahead to recovery. In Rochester, where the worst happened more than a month earlier, Dr. George P. Sayre, a pathologist at Mayo Clinic, gave a check for $2,000 to initiate the Rochester Area Relief Fund, the *Post Bulletin* reported on April 17. Sayre said the money was intended to inspire flood-relief gifts from others in the area. He said that for every $5 donated by someone else, he would match it with a $1 gift, meaning he hoped his $2,000 check would inspire $10,000 in gifts from others.

Sayre told the *Post Bulletin* he made the gift to "challenge those who are always talking against accepting governmental aid, and then neglecting to give at a local level."

He said he was also motivated to make the gift in recognition of the sandbagging labors that had been performed by teenagers from Rochester in helping residents of Winona. "We adults can't always be on the dikes, but we can send a contribution for relief of suffering," Sayre said.

Robert Withers, publisher of the *Post Bulletin*, said: "We hope that this significant act by Dr. Sayre will move thousands in the area to send a gift to the flood relief fund. As important as the money is, equally important is the encouragement it will give to flood victims. It is important that the communities along the Mississippi have evidence that their neighbors stand back of them in this time of trial."

On April 17, Andrella Hansen wrote: "We almost lost everything! Two pumps quit we are exhausted the water will come up one more foot. We just can't do it. Leo won't give up. He is sending over another pump. It is a four-inch and does a wonderful job. More bags. Worked till 1:30 tonight."

The next day, the Hansens went to church. Their son Buzz, who lived in Rochester, went home for the first time in fifteen days. She noted that the water crested at 20.87 feet.

Boats of all types were used to provide transportation through the deep floodwaters. *Courtesy of the Goodhue County Historical Society.*

On Tuesday, April 20, a break opened in the dike at Hansen's Harbor. It had the potential for total disaster, but John Flueger of Red Wing was headed to the harbor with a bulldozer. Andrella wrote: "Almost lost it again today. Flueger's dozer got here just in time today and dropped a load of dirt just in the right place at just the right moment. More sandbags."

DEEP WATER

The Mississippi River crested at St. Paul on April 16 at 26.01 feet, according to the Minnesota Department of Natural Resources. At Red Wing, the river crested at 20.89 feet on April 18. The National Weather Service reported that at Lake City, the river crested at 22.18 feet on April 19. Record levels were set on the same day in Wabasha and Winona.

At Lake City, the river went above flood stage of sixteen feet on April 12. The next day, it reached moderate flood stage of eighteen feet, and by April 15, it exceeded major flood stage of twenty feet, according to the National Weather Service. The river remained above flood stage until May 2, twenty-one days after the flooding started. The river remained within three feet of flood stage until mid-June.

"On April 19 the Mississippi River crested at 20.05 feet at Wabasha," according to the U.S. Department of the Interior.

> *The crest was eight feet over flood stage and 3.3 feet higher than the previous maximum which occurred in 1952. Wabasha became an island as the rampaging waters inundated a third of the city and encircled a large part of it. U.S. Highway 61, the main route through Wabasha, was closed for over a week, and Minnesota State Highway 60, leading to the interstate bridge and Nelson, Wis., was also closed. Water was almost two feet deep over U.S. Highway 61 in town and a greater depth occurred south of town. Highway 60, at the railroad underpass, was flooded to a depth of almost seven feet. Heavy ice floes from Lake Pepin, just upstream from Wabasha, and from the Chippewa River in Wisconsin threatened the town. An ice floe, almost as wide as the river and a quarter of a mile long, smashed into a wooded area above town splintering and grinding the trees which absorbed its impact.*

As a result of the 1952 flood, Wabasha had raised the Wabasha-Nelson dike by four feet. The 1965 flood washed away some three thousand feet of that raise.

The river at Wabasha reached flood stage of twelve feet on April 10. It then passed moderate flood stage of fourteen feet on April 13 and major flood stage of sixteen feet on April 14. It remained above flood stage until May 5, which was twenty-six days of flooding, according to the National Weather Service.

MUCH OF THE CITY of Winona is low-lying ground, prime for flooding. City officials had been watching the crests recorded by other communities upstream and knew similar numbers were awaiting them.

The solution seemed to be a long dike. They dug holes around the city and moved enough earth to build a nine-mile dike around the city.

As the river crested in Winona on April 19 at 20.77 feet, the dike system held and prevented massive damage to the community.

"If we had let it come just the way it wanted to," said Winona mayor R.K. Ellings in the *Daily Republican Eagle*, "we would have been eighty percent under water. Our town is dry."

Winona appeared to be an underwater city when the Mississippi River crested on April 19, 1965, at 20.7 feet above flood stage. Peerless Chain and Bay State Milling companies can be seen surrounded by water, along with parts of East Second Street. *Courtesy of the Winona County Historical Society.*

Ellings added that the city had holes all over from where the dirt was moved. "We can fill them anytime," he said.

Flood stage is fourteen feet in Winona. The Department of the Interior reported that the river in Winona remained at or above that stage for twenty-four days. The flood prevented all rail and air travel to Winona, and Max Conrad Airport was inundated.

"Volunteer workers in Winona waged a tremendous battle against the flood," the Department of the Interior wrote. "There was much at stake. Had Winona's dike system failed, only two small islands would have remained above water. The flood-fighting effort was costly, about $2.6 million, but it probably prevented about $20 million in damages."

With the crest past and people feeling more hopeful, the *Winona Daily News* gave readers a summary that showed the dramatic rise of the waters of the Mississippi River from April 1 to the beginning of the drop.

April 1 – 5.39	April 11 – 13.33
April 2 – 5.95	April 12 – 13.96
April 3 – 6.58	April 13 – 14.52
April 4 – 6.95	April 14 – 15.71
April 5 – 7.88	April 15 – 17.26
April 6 – 9.02	April 16 – 18.79
April 7 – 10.11	April 17 – 19.25
April 8 – 10.85	April 18 – 19.91
April 9 – 12.08	April 19 – 20.75
April 10 – 12.60	April 20 – 20.69

Winona reached flood stage of thirteen feet on April 10, moderate flood stage of fifteen feet on April 13 and major flood stage of eighteen feet on April 16. The river stayed above flood stage until May 5, which was twenty-six days of flood-level waters. The river held close to flood stage until mid-June, according to the National Weather Service.

Just downstream from Winona and across the river, the city of La Crosse had been cut in two by water spilling over Causeway Boulevard, the main route through the city, causing travelers to make a detour of several miles if they wanted to go from the north side of town to the south side, or vice versa. The flood crested in La Crosse at 17.96 feet on April 22, which was 2.6 feet higher than the 1952 flood.

The Lake Center Switch Company buildings at Johnson and Front Streets, near the river channel in Winona, show the extent of the floodwaters. *Courtesy of the Winona County Historical Society.*

"In La Crosse and its environs, over 600 homes and about eighty businesses were flooded. Over 1,200 persons were evacuated from their homes," according to the Department of the Interior. "Total damages at La Crosse, including the cost of flood fighting, were about $7.6 million; no other municipality except Dubuque, Iowa, suffered greater damage."

THE FLOOD HAD CRESTED in each city, but the drama was not over. Hundreds of people had been evacuated, and they desperately wanted to return home. Businesses had been closed or trimmed back, and they wanted to move ahead. But the water, which rose so slowly and steadily, started down with the same unhurried pace. The Mississippi River began, as the *Daily Republican Eagle* called it, "a withdrawal almost as dramatic as its rise."

Residents all along the river had spent most of two weeks preparing for and battling the flood. Now, as it receded, they became restless. As the water retreated, it deposited the debris it had been carrying. It had picked up anything in its path and now dropped those items miles downstream from where they originated. Property from homes and garages and yards were dumped along the way.

ON APRIL 21, ANDRELLA Hansen wrote in her diary that the river dropped seven inches. That was good news, but then, as if a record flood had not been challenging enough, she added news that Lawrence Peterson, a longtime friend of their family, had died of a heart attack, and Alice Hansen, another friend, was in the hospital from a heart attack. "So much trouble," Andrella wrote.

The next day, Elmer Bengsten, a friend from Red Wing, stayed with the boys while the Hansens went to the Peterson funeral. Andrella summed up the time, writing, "We're terribly tired."

On April 23, she noted that the water had gone down another eighteen inches, progress that she called an "agonizingly slow drop."

Her next entries focus only on the receding water.

April 24 – Water 18.2 feet
April 25 – Water 17.7 feet
April 26 – Water 17 feet
April 27 – Water 16.5 feet
April 28 – Water 16 feet

Over the next two days, the Hansens tried to return to a normal life. Andrella went for a haircut. They moved furniture back into place. They replaced docks and began the long process of cleaning the buildings and area.

On May 1, there is relief in her tone when she writes, "The river is about fourteen feet, and I guess we are saved now. The Lord was willing that we should be OK. By the grace of God and much help from our friends and neighbors and our three sons, we will be back in business shortly."

The Hansens reported in the *Daily Republican Eagle* that they had used five thousand cubic yards of dirt to build the dike, which was eight hundred feet long and nine feet high, that surrounded their main building. In preparation for the flood, they had moved sixteen cruisers from thirty to forty-two feet in length and twenty smaller boats to safer ground, and those boats needed to be returned to the water. The Hansens hoped they could be fully back in business by June 1.

WHEN THE HANSENS OPENED the harbor in 1952, it was just a small pond on the side of the river. They made access into the pond and then constructed the buildings for the business. At the time of the flood, they had been in business for thirteen years, and the month-long battle against the water was exhausting. They watched as the waters rose up over the banks and through their parking lot almost to the edge of Highway 61, hoping their family business would survive. It did.

Pete, their son who came home from college to help during the spring and summer of 1965, took over the business in 1972 and ran it for about twenty-five years before his son Allen, who owns it now, took over. In the years since the flood of 1965, the Hansens have added more buildings and docks to their marina. They raised the level of the natural dike to add more protection from high-water years.

"We wanted to make sure that everything is either elevated, or can get wet and not be damaged," said Allen, who has spent his entire life, except for college in Iowa and a time in the U.S. Army Reserve, living and working at Hansen's Harbor.

Born in 1969, Allen wasn't alive for the 1965 flood, but he heard the family stories and has seen other high- and low-water years.

"Can you imagine how much water it takes to raise Lake Pepin one inch?" he asked. "And then, as the water level rises, the lake gets wider as water flows into the backwaters and spreads out through the valleys. It's fifty miles between the locks, so when the water goes up and down several feet, that's an incredible amount of water."

9

THE MISSISSIPPI RIVER LEAVES ITS MARKS

Disasters have always brought out the curiosity in human beings. The Flood of 1965 was no exception. At the height of the flooding, Governor Karl Rovaag warned amateur photographers to stay out of flood areas and not take unnecessary chances to take pictures, according to the *Post Bulletin*. Similarly, Lake City mayor Harry Johnson asked that persons stay away from Lake City unless they were on official business, because motorists wanting to view floodwaters were causing problems for trucks trying to deliver emergency supplies.

GRADUALLY, NORMAL ACTIVITIES RESUMED along the banks of the Mississippi River. The Chicago Great Western Railway sent a freight train with thirty-seven cars carrying vital supplies for Red Wing industries on April 24. Two days later, the Milwaukee Road ran the first passenger train, and on April 27, full rail service was resumed.

By April 26, the river had dropped to a level of seventeen feet at Red Wing, still three feet over flood stage, but low enough that Highway 63, which had been closed for ten days, could reopen. Workers could stop using the improvised ferry to get from Wisconsin to Red Wing and their jobs.

Always a concern for Minnesota residents is the start of the spring fishing season, and the *Winona Daily News* assured readers that the season would get under way on May 1. "Thirty thousand fishable size brown trout from the Lanesboro trout hatchery have been stocked in the trout streams and creeks of ten Southeastern Minnesota counties during the past two weeks for Saturday's opening," it reported.

Although waters were still high in many places, in general, the Mississippi River had dropped four feet from the crest by the start of the fishing season. Those fishing from boats would need to watch for flood debris, and Winona sheriff George Fort, in charge of the river patrol in the Winona area, lifted the ban on riverboats, although he cautioned boaters to stay away from sandbag dikes and to use care. Some harbors and marinas remained closed because of damage from the flooding.

Russell Hanson, state supervisor of fisheries in Southeast Minnesota, said that the early bad weather and the flooding had taken a toll on fish during the winter and spring, but the *Daily News* noted that "heavily fished streams are stocked several times each season."

DENNIS M. JAWSON, THE state relations director for the Red Cross, reported to Governor Rolvaag that 1,831 dwellings had been destroyed or damaged in Minnesota. Jawson noted that 4,179 families had suffered losses and that 21,000 persons would be affected by the flood before the waters fully receded. He added that 28,500 disaster victims and flood workers had received Red Cross care and that $36,441 had been spent by the Red Cross in the Mankato area on emergency care.

THE *DAILY REPUBLICAN EAGLE* noted: "The mighty Mississippi has returned to its banks, but the marks it left during its destructive fling will be visible for a long time. Much of the mud has been washed out of the flooded homes and business establishments, but warped floors and doors, peeling wallpaper and falling plaster serve as grim reminders of the merciless water that rose to heights no one believed possible."

The waters receded over days and weeks, leaving behind a path of destruction that would take months or years to repair and restore. Knowing the true extent of the damage would take months, and the cost to businesses along the river would be an astounding number.

Northern State Power Company estimated losses at $2 million to the plants it owned along the Mississippi River.

One Red Wing business manager told the *Daily Republican Eagle*: "We'll never know just how hard it hit us. Production losses from something like this can hardly be made up."

The Wisconsin end of the Red Wing bridge is inundated by the Mississippi River. *Courtesy of the Goodhue County Historical Society.*

The National Weather Service reported that the flood caused $225 million in damages with $173 million happening along the main stem of the Mississippi River.

DAN FOLEY, WHO DIRECTED flood-control efforts in Wabasha, told the *Rochester Post-Bulletin*, "This experience focuses attention on the pressing need for legislation and appropriation of funds for more efficient flood control on a permanent basis."

James R. Smith, vice president of the Mississippi Valley Association, felt the same and took his case to subcommittees on public works of the U.S. House and Senate committees on appropriations in Washington.

"Nowhere on the American continent has there ever been a more graphic demonstration that the price of flood protection can never be as high as the price of property damage when a major flood strikes," Smith testified. "The American people will pay for flood protection whether they get it or not. Much of the damage could have been prevented had the Upper Mississippi Valley had a truly valley-wide flood control program."

He continued: "The damage of the 1965 flood in the Upper Mississippi Valley must not be permitted to happen again. Congress should undertake immediately an accelerated program of study to work out a real flood protection program for that region."

Smith, on behalf of the Mississippi Valley Association, urged the committees to provide $1 million to fund a study of levees, flood walls and storage reservoirs.

He explained that such a study should "include full consideration of the problems of cities on tributary streams as well as the ability of those tributaries to reduce flows on the main stem of the Mississippi. Such a study should determine whether the existence of a valley-wide flood control program would reduce the cost of local flood protection projects not yet constructed."

Smith also let the committees know that the Mississippi Valley Association had scheduled a conference in Burlington, Iowa, on June 23, to develop recommended actions to take against future flood disasters.

In a May 25 guest editorial in the *Winona Daily News*, Albert Marshall urged further actions to prevent similar floods in the future. "The fact that floods are inevitable under circumstances similar to those existing this past winter and spring does not, in the opinion of many students of the subject, lessen the need for formulating programs designed to prevent future floods of possibly even greater magnitude," he wrote.

Marshall said having communities like Mankato and Winona build dikes and levees based on the 1965 flood might only leave them vulnerable when a larger flood came along.

He wrote that increased efforts to hold back water runoff would be a major step in the right direction, and he quoted Governor Rolvaag as saying, "I am compelled to point out that flood damage has been greatly accentuated by ignoring a fundamental concept of conservation—the vital necessity of holding as much water as possible on the land near the point where it falls."

Marshall explained that in Minnesota, many acres of wetlands had been drained to create farmlands, resulting in higher runoff rates and reduced wildlife habitat, in spite of a surplus of existing farmland.

He concluded by calling for state and federal agencies to make "changes in present incentive programs administered by the federal government to insure that federal funds are spent in all instances to aid and stimulate rather than obstruct or delay constructive conservation."

WALL OF WATER

"After the 1952 flood, they said it couldn't happen again in 100 years, but the rivers don't respect the law of averages."

That's how the *Winona Daily News* introduced an article published on May 27, 1965, reflecting on the flood of 1965. The unnamed author took a poetic view of how the many factors that caused the flood came to be.

> *Spawned in tiny puddles of freshly-melted snow in the headwaters of the mighty Mississippi River basin, and fed by swollen streams along its upper reaches, a flood that threatened the very life of Winona was born.*
>
> *The gigantic wall of water that pounded at the dikes protecting the city may have started in a small glen in far-western Minnesota and followed the course of the Minnesota River to the Mississippi at St. Paul, or it might have been a little lake in the Itasca State Park area feeding into the very source of the Mississippi or still again it could have been water from the heavy snows of Northern and Western Wisconsin moving into the headwaters of the St. Croix or the Chippewa rivers.*

These early beginnings led to what the writer called the "most advertised-in-advance flood in the history of Winona."

The power of the floodwaters is evident in this section of railroad track outside of Red Wing. *Courtesy of the Goodhue County Historical Society.*

The writer remembered the reports of snow: twenty-seven inches in St. Cloud, fifteen inches in Duluth, followed by the late February warming that sent snow, ice and water into the streams that were all heading to the Mississippi River to create the flood that lasted for weeks, topped the flood of 1952 and defied the law of averages.

CLEANUP AFTER THE FLOOD affected not only the residents along the Mississippi River and its tributaries, but also the U.S. Army Corps of Engineers, which is charged with maintaining the nine-foot commercial navigation channel at all times.

Captain Allen W. Fiedler, in charge of the dredge boat *William A. Thompson*, estimated that four million cubic yards of sand and gravel needed to be removed from the river. Fiedler told the *Winona Daily News* that on his first trip down the river after the flood, he saw sandbars at almost every bend and that he was receiving reports of towboats being stuck in places where no sandbars had been reported before.

"We have about four times the normal amount of maintenance pumping to do this year because of the flood," Fiedler told the *Daily News*. "There have been many changes in the river channel, new islands have been formed, old ones have disappeared, deep holes filled, shorelines scooped out and a lot of underwater changes."

The *Thompson* carried a crew of sixty-five and had them working four rotating shifts, eight hours each, around the clock and seven days a week. The twenty-inch dredge pipe worked nonstop, except when the *Thompson* was moving from one sandbar to the next.

RECEDING WATER

In the aftermath of the flood, some critics blamed at least some of the effects of the flooding on the U.S. Army Corps of Engineers and the dams it had built in the 1930s.

At a meeting in Prairie du Chien, Wisconsin, sponsored by the corps of engineers to allow it to hear local views, citizens expressed concern that flood-control projects upstream had made things worse for them. They stated that keeping the river high enough for commercial navigation contributed to the higher levels of water during the flood.

The *Winona Daily News* reported that Robert Cowan of St. Paul explained that if Pool 9 north of Prairie du Chien were completely empty, the water flow of 278,000 cubic feet per second at the height of the 1965 flood would have filled the pool three times each day.

AT THE HEIGHT OF the flood, many streets in Wabasha were underwater and postmen delivered mail by boat, reported the *Winona Daily News*. The city recovered and by February had resumed plans for community improvements, including a nine-hole golf course at Coffee Mill Bluff, a new library, a new motel and a recreation center, according to Dean Plank, secretary of the chamber of commerce.

Wabasha mayor Ray Young predicted that the golf course, featuring an octagon-shaped clubhouse, would be the biggest development in the town in 1966. "City planning is necessary to develop these areas," he said, "as well as areas along the waterfront and a downtown sidewalk, curb and gutter program."

OTHER DEVELOPMENTS IN THE wake of the flood were not as pleasant. Gilbert Erickson from Lindstrom, Minnesota, had been repairing damaged railroad right-of-way on May 7, 1965, when the boat that he and three other workers were using floated into some debris and tipped. Erickson was presumed drowned, but searches for his body were unsuccessful, according to the *Winona Daily News*.

Then, on August 2, 1966, fifteen months later, George Lipinski from Buffalo City was fishing in the backwaters and saw a boot floating on the water. He moved closer and discovered a body, which turned out to be Erickson's.

Lipinski went to Fountain City and called the Buffalo County Sheriff's Office. Officers went to the location and found Erickson, his left side and leg floating in the water and his right leg buried in the sand. They found his wallet with identification and credit card under his body. They took Erickson to the Colby Funeral Home in Fountain City.

AS COULD BE EXPECTED, the flood of 1965 created debt for many communities along the Mississippi River and its tributaries. With President Johnson designating much of Minnesota a disaster area, funds were available, but in some cases they didn't cover everything and were often slow in being distributed.

In February 1967, Winona mayor R.K. Ellings told the city council that some of the federal funds promised to the city were being held back by the Office of Emergency Planning because it had not received approval from the state agency to release the money.

The mayor reported that flood bills of $1,760,425 were eligible for reimbursement and that the city had received $1,390,000 in disaster grants, according to the *Winona Daily News*. The city considered issuing bonds to help make up the difference until the remaining funding could be received.

Later that month, Ellings decided to talk with Minnesota senators Walter Mondale and Eugene McCarthy as well as Vice President Hubert Humphrey to see if they could help with the situation.

Humans weren't the only living beings affected by the flood. In an article published on March 30, 1969, Lefty Hymes, outdoor writer for the *Winona Daily News*, reviewed a report titled *Observations on the Effects of the 1965 Flood on Upper Mississippi River Wildlife and Fish* from the staff of the Upper Mississippi River Wildlife and Fish Refuge.

"Animal life succumbing direct to the floods cannot be adequately observed and tabulated," the report stated. "Carcasses are swept away by the flood waters or lodged beneath driftwood, silt or sand deposits. Predation and natural deterioration of animals destroyed by drowning results in the rapid disappearance of many specimens succumbing directly to the flood. Observers are hampered from conducting detailed observation by hazards of the flood and many other factors."

Hymes noted that even water mammals such as muskrat, beaver and raccoon—all capable swimmers—were often taken by the flood. Animals less likely to try swimming were forced away from the rivers and tributaries and often pushed onto higher ground, including highways and railroad tracks, where many of them died, not by drowning, but by collisions with cars and trains.

Many animals in the study were found on islands. They had either been pushed there by floodwaters or were on islands and then could not escape during the weeks of high water levels.

"Normal floods come during the litter time of [muskrats]," Hymes wrote. "Temporary nests are commonly found in the fork of trees with many of the blind young, dead from exposure. Floods have no respect of age."

Ducks, geese and swans were able to deal with the flood better than many of the legged creatures, and Hymes stated that they "gathered by the tens of thousands in the Weaver bottomlands during the 1965 flood, feeding from the flooded fields."

Birds that build low nests often have their homes destroyed by floods, but they quickly rebuild in new locations, Hymes wrote. He added that reptiles and amphibians seem unaffected by the flood.

Hymes stated that one of the conclusions of the report regarding animals affected by the flood said, "Direct effects of flooding are the drowning of trapped animals, the driving of females from usual habitat during the critical breeding and rearing period, and forcing of wildlife populations into unsuitable range where excessive predation or starvation may result."

THE WATERS RECEDED OVER days and weeks, leaving behind a path of destruction. Homes and businesses had been damaged. Cars had been swamped. Personal property had floated down the raging river. Lives had been lost.

Communities faced significant debt as they worked to rebuild. Organizations and individuals stepped up to provide money and labor to help their fellow citizens get their lives back in order.

On the Mississippi River and its tributaries, the flood crests of 1965 stand as records to this day, most more than a foot higher than the second-highest crest in most locations, according to the National Weather Service.

The fearful buildup and the agonizing retreat of the 1965 flood left many people devastated. The *Daily Republican Eagle* wrote: "For thousands of Mississippi River bank residents the word flood will bring to mind 1965. And a combination of the two will bring a shudder to all who witnessed the massive silent siege."

ABOUT THE AUTHOR

Author Steve Gardiner aboard his boat on Lake Pepin. *Photo by Peggy Gardiner.*

Steve Gardiner taught high school English and journalism for thirty-eight years in Wyoming, Peru and Montana. He was the 2008 Montana Teacher of the Year and is a National Board Certified Teacher. He holds a doctorate of education degree. He has published articles in the *New York Times*, the *Chicago Tribune*, the *Christian Science Monitor*, the *Denver Post*, *Educational Leadership*, *Phi Delta Kappan*, *Education Week* and many other publications.

After retiring from teaching, he worked as a reporter for the *Red Wing Republican Eagle* for three years. His most recent books are *Adventure Relativity: When Intense Experiences Shift Time* (2020) and *Mountain Dreams: The Drive to Explore, Experience, and Expand* (2021). Read more at www.quietwaterpublishing.com.

Steve and his wife, Peggy, live in Lake City and enjoy hiking, biking and boating on Lake Pepin with their grandsons.

Visit us at
www.historypress.com